WHAT PEOPLE A

PAGAN PORT/
GODDESSES

Morgan Daimler is my 'go to' guide for anything in regard to Irish Paganism and this book will be added to my growing collection of her wonderful works that I use regularly for reference. It covers any and every Irish deity you could think of and some that you may not have heard about; this book details them all. Fascinating stories and histories for each deity including correspondences, symbols and sources of reference give comprehensive and 'all you need to know' information. Highly recommended.

Rachel Patterson, author of *Pagan Portals – The Cailleach, Arc of the Goddess, The Art of Ritual* and other witchcraft titles

Morgan Daimler has written an excellent brief introduction to the deities of Ireland in an accessible encyclopedic format. She offers a compilation of information about many deities, and includes scholarly sources for each one, as well as brief suggestions for offerings and interacting with the deities for those who are just beginning their journey into Irish spirituality. Highly recommended.

Erynn Rowan Laurie, author of *Ogam: Weaving Word Wisdom* and *The Well of Five Streams: Essays on Celtic Paganism*

This book is a needed reference work, giving essential information on their pantheon to the Irish Pagan community. It will no doubt be treasured by generations of readers.

Segomâros Widugeni, formerly **Aedh Rua**, author of *Celtic Flame*

In *Pagan Portals: Gods and Goddesses of Ireland*, Morgan Daimler has provided a comprehensive study of the pagan deities of

Ireland and put them in their proper context – rather than merely a collection of 'Celtic' Gods. The Gods of Ireland are a complex bunch and the detail she has condensed into this little book offers valuable access for those who are daunted by more academic offerings when what they are looking for is concise information. The wild scenery of Ireland hints at highly magical places and the author has managed to convey this air of mysticism with these tantalising glimpses of the deities who ruled, fought and loved their way across the mountains, glens and lakes of the landscape. Highly recommended for all who would follow in their footsteps.
Mélusine Draco, author of the *Traditional Witchcraft* series and *The Secret People*

Daimler's book is a perfect resource for anyone beginning to research and honour Irish deities. She includes information, not only about the more familiar Goddesses and Gods but also the less well known, such as Medb and Crom Cruach.

Written in the style of an encyclopedia, the book is accessible to readers who want basic information and for those who wish to delve deeper, there is an excellent section offering suggestions for further reading.

As always Morgan Daimler's writing is clear, concise, thoroughly researched and a pleasure to read. This is the book that I was looking for twenty years ago!
Jane Brideson, artist and blogger at The Ever-Living Ones – Irish Goddesses & Gods in Landscape, Myth & Custom

Pagan Portals

Gods and Goddesses of Ireland

A Guide to Irish Deities

Pagan Portals
Gods and Goddesses of Ireland

A Guide to Irish Deities

Morgan Daimler

MOON BOOKS

Winchester, UK
Washington, USA

JOHN HUNT PUBLISHING

First published by Moon Books, 2016
Moon Books is an imprint of John Hunt Publishing Ltd., No. 3 East Street, Alresford
Hampshire SO24 9EE, UK
office@jhpbooks.net
www.johnhuntpublishing.com
www.moon-books.net

For distributor details and how to order please visit the 'Ordering' section on our website.

Text copyright: Morgan Daimler 2016

ISBN: 978 1 78279 315 1
978 1 78535 450 2 (ebook)
Library of Congress Control Number: 2016949320

A CIP catalogue record for this book is available from the British Library.

Design: Stuart Davies

UK: Printed and bound by CPI Group (UK) Ltd, Croydon, CR0 4YY
Printed in North America by CPI GPS partners

We operate a distinctive and ethical publishing philosophy in all
areas of our business, from our global network of authors to
production and worldwide distribution.

CONTENTS

This book is dedicated to Maya who has always encouraged me;
thank you mo chara.
And to Lora O'Brien for making me think to include
Medb of Connacht.

Acknowledgements

With thanks to everyone who has supported me through my writing, especially my family. I'd also like to thank the people who responded on my Facebook author page with suggestions for which deities they most wanted to see in a book like this; I hope I included as many of them as possible.

Author's Note

There are many books available on the Celtic Gods more generally and a few on the Irish Gods specifically, but none, to my knowledge, that try to do what I am aiming to do here – concisely describe a variety of Irish Gods in one easy-to-use reference. The motivation for this is simply to give people a needed resource and make the information more readily available. This book was written as a resource for seekers that will offer both solid academic material and suggestions for further reading in a format that is accessible and designed to be easy to read. This book is not by any means a complete or in-depth listing of every single Irish deity, nor of everything we know about the Gods that are listed, but rather is meant to provide a concise basic reference with the highlights of important information. The Irish Gods are complex and often have a variety of myths associated with them, which are layered and full of nuances.

In writing this I have drawn on many different sources and have carefully referenced and cited all of them in notes at the end of each entry. While this book can and does serve as a stand-alone work, ideally I hope that the reader will be drawn to learn more and decide to continue seeking. To help with this I have provided a list of both the references I used in my writing and also of recommended further reading at the end of the book under the bibliography. I have tried to offer books that represent an array of options for people, with different viewpoints and approaches to honoring the Irish Gods and to understanding who they were and are.

I have been an Irish pagan since 1991 and actively honoring the Irish Gods for more than 25 years at this point; I am a priestess of the Goddess Macha, tutelary deity of Ulster. I have found a profound spiritual value in honoring these Gods and in studying their history and mythology as well as learning how to connect to them in a modern context. For some people this book may be the first step in a life long journey studying or honoring the Irish Gods; others may find that they don't call to you in that way, but nonetheless something valuable can be gained here. Ultimately no knowledge is ever wasted.

Introduction – Who are the Irish Gods?

Rooted in the past, but still active in the world today, the Gods of Ireland have always been powerful forces that can bless or challenge, but often the most difficult thing is to simply find information about them. This short introduction looks at a variety of different Irish deities, from their ancient roots to the modern practices associated with honoring them in an encyclopedia-style book with entries in easy-to-use sections.

The Irish Gods have long been one of the most popular groups among modern pagans and yet finding good information on them can be difficult. Often they are simply lumped in with the other Celtic Gods creating a false sense of a unified Pan-Celtic pantheon that never existed historically. Another common problem stemming from this same approach is that only the most popular Gods, or those about whom we have the most information, tend to be written about in the readily available pagan resources, but the less popular or more obscure deities are left out. What material can be found is unfortunately not always the most reliable either, and many books freely blend fact with fiction in a way that can be very confusing to readers. The end result is that someone interested in Irish paganism, especially when they are just beginning, may find it difficult to find the information they are looking for and to sort out quality information from invention.

The way this particular book is set up we will look at a brief summary of a variety of different deities, rather like a small encyclopedia, with basic information given for each one including the meaning of their name, who they are related to, what they are associated with, and any available mythology. For ease of use I've divided the book into three main sections: Gods of the Tuatha Dé Danann, Goddesses of the Tuatha Dé Danann, and Other Irish Deities. My choice to do this was based mostly in the view that the Tuatha Dé Danann are the main deities of Ireland, but we do also see other Gods who are not included among the Tuatha Dé Danann that are important. The decision to choose to divide Gods and Goddesses is also intended to make the book easier to use. Unfortunately, due to the size of this book, it's impossible to include every single Irish deity in any depth so instead I will try to offer a wider selection than is usually found in most other books and include as much information about each deity as possible.

For those who are interested in a particular deity who is not listed in this short work I suggest looking to the books used as references for this one, particularly Daithi O hOgain's *Lore of Ireland* and MacKillop's *Dictionary of Celtic Mythology*. That said, however, please keep in mind that even the best academic text often omits the deities for whom we have the most limited amount of information and in some cases there is little choice but to go directly to the original source material and look for whatever hints you can find, although in many cases that may be only a single line in one story. For example, we have no extant Irish moon deity in the original mythology, although there are hints and clues to several potential candidates.

The Irish Gods survived in mythology written down after conversion and then later in folklore, tied as strongly as they were to particular locations. They are woven into the very landscape of Ireland, to the island's history and spirit, to the mounds and the sacred places. They are the Gods of the pagans and, some say, they are the Gentry (fairies) of the Christians, changing as the world around them changes yet always remaining in the heartbeat of the land itself and the imagination of the people.

Chapter 1

The Tuatha Dé Danann: Gods

Aengus

Also called Aongus, Aonghus, or Angus, and Oengus in Old Irish, and given the epithet of Mac ind Og (the young son), Mac in Dá Oc (son of the two young ones), or Aonghus an Bhroga (Angus of the Brugh). In old Irish his name breaks down to óen, 'unique, without equal', and gus, 'force or vigor'[1] giving us a meaning of 'unique force' or 'unequaled vigor'.

His father is the Dagda, and his mother is the Goddess Bóinn, eponymous deity of the Boyne river; he was the product of an affair between the two, which the Dagda hid from Bóinn's husband, Elcmar, by causing a single day and night to last for nine months[2]. Because of this Aengus was, technically, conceived and born on the same day, which is considered the source of his epithet 'the young son'. Through his father's side he has many siblings including the Goddess Brighid. He is said to have at least one daughter, Maga, and through her to be connected to the ancestry of the royal house of Ulster[3].

Smyth conjectures that Aengus was conceived at Samhain, and because his birth was hidden and that he was also born on Samhain[4]. Samhain is a holiday that has other associations for Aengus as well, as it is also the day that he is finally able to obtain the one woman he most desires. This occurs in the Aislinge Oenguso, which tells of how Aengus began dreaming of a mysterious woman, Caer Iobharmheith (Caer Ibormeith in Old Irish), and fell into a wasting sickness; after help from his mother and father finally revealed the woman's identity he found her on Samhain, wooed her, and the two flew off in the form of swans[5].

His home is possibly the most famous of all the fairy mounds, the Brugh na Bóinne, which he won through trickery. There are different versions of the story of how he managed this, one being that he tricked the Brugh away from Elcmar with the help of his father, the Dagda, while in another the Dagda is the owner of the Brugh and it is from him that Aengus obtains the Brugh, either through his own cleverness or with the help of one of his foster fathers. The basis of the story remains the same, however, in that Aengus arrives at the Brugh and asks its owner to be given the place for a day and night. This is granted, but when the original owner asks for the Brugh back 24 hours later Aengus responds that since all time is divided by day and night the Brugh is now his. In this way he successfully wins the place that is best known as his.

Aengus is generally viewed as a God of youth, beauty, and love, and is known in the myths and folklore to aid lovers, most famously Dairmait and Grainne in the Fenian Cycle[6]. He is also known as a clever God, as evidenced by his winning of the Brugh, and an incident in the *Cath Maige Tuired* where he advises his father, the Dagda, on how to trick the unfair king Bres into paying him what he is justly owed for his work.

He has several important possessions, including a magical horse so large it can carry an entire household, and who created Lough Neagh when it urinated, and a multicolored cloak that appears to be of a single color to the eyes of someone about to die[7]. It is said that four white birds circle his head, which are either swans or his own kisses shape-changed.

Modern practitioners may choose to connect to Aengus for a variety of reasons, but he is often appealed to as a deity of love. Offerings to him might include milk, beer, or good food, as well as anything else the practitioner feels most appropriate.

1. eDIL, n.d.
2. Smyth, 1988
3. MacKillop, 1998
4. Smyth, 1988

5. Shaw, 1934
6. MacKillop, 1998
7. O hOgain, 2006

Credne

Called Credne or Creidne in Old Irish and Creidhne in modern Irish. He is given the epithet 'Cerd' meaning craftsman or artisan and was known to work with bronze, brass, and gold[1]. He is described as the 'wright' of the Gods and is often listed with his two brothers, Goibniu the blacksmith and Luchta the carpenter; the three together are called the three Gods of skill of the Tuatha Dé Danann. After Nuada, High King of the Tuatha Dé Danann, lost his arm in the first battle of Maige Tuired it was Credne who helped the physician God Dian Cécht fashion a replacement arm of silver for him[2]. During the battle with the Fomorians Credne aided the TDD along with his brothers by furnishing the Gods with weapons, his particular contribution being the spear rivets, sword hilts, and shield bosses and rims[3].

His symbols might include the tools of metalsmithing: a small hammer, awl, or a center punch, for example. Offerings to Credne may include water, ale, or any precious or semi-precious metal.

1. MacKillop, 1998
2. Macalister, R., 1941
3. MacKillop, 1998

Dagda

One of the most well known Gods of the Tuatha Dé Danann is the Dagda. He can be found under many variations of the name and under many by-names, such as Daghdae, Dagdai, Daghdo, Daghdou, Dagdae, Dagdhua, Dagdhae, Dagda Mor, Dagda Donn and Eochaid Ollathair, Ruad Rofessa, Aedh Alainn, Aodh Ruadh Ro-fessa; usually the definitive article 'the' is added before Dagda[1]. The name Dagda itself is an epithet that means 'Good

God', implying a God good at all things. This name is gained during the second battle of Maige Tuired when he promises to do as much as all the other Tuatha Dé have said they will do in the fight[2]. His by-names tell us a great deal about him as well: Eochaid Ollathair 'Father of Many', Ruad Rofessa 'Red man of Knowledge' (specifically Druidic or Occult), Aedh Alainn 'Fiery Lustrous One'[3]. People inclined to look at the Dagda as a more neopagan type Father God should bear in mind the actual connotations of 'Good God' as well as the more restricted translation of Ollathair, as there is no direct evidence that he was previously seen as the literal father of the Gods, but rather as prolific. In fairness to that view, however, O hOgain does suggest that the Dagda can be connected to the 'Dis Pater' father deity that Caesar claims the Gauls believed they descended from[4]. Additionally the text of the *Cath Maige Tuired* provides a long list of names for the Dagda, after he is challenged to give a ride to a Fomorian princess and replies that he has a geas preventing him doing so unless she knows his full name. She asks him three times for his name and on the third request he replies: 'Fer Benn Bruach Brogaill Broumide Cerbad Caic Rolaig Builc Labair Cerrce Di Brig Oldathair Boith Athgen mBethai Brightere Tri Carboid Roth Rimaire Riog Scotbe Obthe Olaithbe'[5]. O hOgain suggests the name Dagda comes from the root Dago-Dewios, a cognate with other Indo-European sky Gods such as Zeus, and also through this and his imagery to the Gaulish Secullos[6].

In some sources the Dagda is said to be the son of Elatha and married to the Morrigan, although he is also known to have fathered at least one child with Boinn. His children vary by source, but are usually given as Aengus mac Og, Cearmait, Aodh Caomh, Conan, Midir, Bodhbh Dearg, Ainge, and Brighid; in one later example Dian Cécht is also said to be his son[7]. His sons often die after trying to obtain a woman who is not available; only Aengus successfully marries the literal woman of his dreams, Caer Iobharmheith. This may connect the Dagda to the concept of passion or of sexual envy, as he himself fathered Aengus on another man's wife. He is also sometimes said to be the brother of Nuada and Ogma[8].

The Dagda is generally described as being a large man, sometimes comically so, with a tremendous appetite and immense capacity. It was said that to make his porridge he needed 80 gallons of milk as well as several whole sheep, pigs, and goats, and that he ate this meal with a ladle large enough to hold two people lying down[9]. Some modern sources describe him as red-haired, possibly relating to the name Ruad Rofessa, and describe his clothing as a short tunic, sometimes obscenely short. He is considered to be generous, wise, and bigger-than-life in his appetites[10]. He is often described as immensely strong and able to complete great feats such building a fort single-handedly or clearing 12 plains in a single night.

The Book of Lecan states that the Dagda ruled for 80 years as King of the Gods after the death of Lugh, but other sources state that he was killed fighting Ceithlinn at the second battle of Maige Tuired[11]. This is later explained with a story saying that he took a wound in the battle that took 80 years to kill him, but that is clearly an attempt to unify the varying tales into a coherent whole[12]. He was said to be a master of Druidic magic and to possesses several magical objects. It was the Dagda who held the cauldron of abundance brought from Murias, one of the four treasures. He also owned a great club that was so large it had to be dragged on wheels behind him; it is said that one end of the club could kill nine men with one blow, while the other could heal[13]. His horse was Acein (ocean) and the Dagda possessed a harp whose playing changed the seasons. This harp was stolen by the Fomorians, and the Dagda along with Nuada and Ogma had to journey to recover it, possibly indicating its importance to maintaining the order of time and the seasons.

The Dagda is associated with Brugh na Boynne and also with a site in Donegal called Grianan Ailigh as well as Leighead

Lachtmhaighe in Clare, Cnoc Baine in Tyrone and O Chualann in Wicklow[14]. It is said that it was the Dagda who delegated each of the sidhe to the Tuatha Dé after their defeat by the Milesians, possibly at Manannán mac Lir's suggestion[15]. The Dagda originally lived at Newgrange (Burgh na Boynne), but was tricked out of the site by his son Angus. He is also particularly associated with Samhain, when he was said to unite with the Morrigan to gain her assistance for the Tuatha Dé Danann in the coming battle of Maige Tuired; this is also the time that he united with the Fomorian princess, gaining her assistance against her own people in the battle.

In general terms we can associate the Dagda with a variety of things including Druidic magic, wisdom, leadership, fertility, generosity, abundance, and all-around skill. O hOgain relates to him as a God related to the sun and solar imagery, and suggests that we may deduce from descriptions of the Dagda as 'swift' that he was seen as a God who responded quickly to those who prayed to him[15]. Some modern practitioners and scholars see him as a cognate of either the Norse Thor or Odin, with strong arguments for either view; others suggest an association with the Roman Dis Pater or Gaulish Secullos. Many modern Druids may choose to see the Dagda as a God of Druids, and he certainly has a strong connection to Druidic magic.

Offerings to the Dagda might include dark beers or ales as well as porridge, especially mixed with butter and with items like bacon added in. His symbols could be the club or staff and the cauldron.

1. Gray, 1983; O hOgain, 2006
2. Gray, 1983
3. O hOgain, 2006
4. Ibid
5. Gray, 1983
6. O hOgain, 2006

7. Ibid
8. Ibid
9. Berresford Ellis, 1987
10. O hOgain, 2006
11. Smyth, 1988
12. O hOgain, 2006
13. Berresford Ellis, 1987; O hOgain, 2006
14. Smyth, 1988; O hOgain, 2006
15. O hOgain, 2006

Dian Cécht

Also spelled Dían Cécht, Diancécht, Dian Céacht, and later appearing as Mac Cécht[1]. He is an Irish God associated with physicians, healing, and restoring the body. His name seems to mean 'swift traveler' and he is one of the Tuatha Dé Danann who is explicitly called a God in the surviving mythology[2]. Dian Cécht was considered the supreme physician of the Gods and possessed a well or cauldron, the Slaine, into which the wounded could be placed and from which they would emerge restored. Throughout the Irish texts where he appears he is renowned for his healing skill and he is called 'the healing sage of Ireland' and 'God of health'[3].

In the *Lebor Gabala Erenn* we are told that he was the son of Esarg and had three brothers, the crafting Gods Goibhniu, Creidhne, and Luchtne [4]. According to the same source he is the father of two other Irish healing deities, Miach and Airmed, as well as Cu, and Cethan, and in the mythological cycle is referred to as having two other sons who are also healers, likely Ormiach and Ochtriuil. He is also the father of Etan the poetess and Cian and the grandfather of Lugh[5].

He is not only a God of active healing, but also of the knowledge of healing arts and of healing magic. He is known as a superlative healer with any method. We don't have many existing myths featuring Dian Cécht, but the ones we do have generally center on his healing skill in one way or another. He created his great healing well by placing one of every healing herb into it, and in mythology he is known to heal grievous wounds, including replacing Nuada's severed arm with a fully functioning one of silver, and healing Midir's wounded eye, and to cure plagues in the guise of serpents[6]. There is a reference in the St. Gall's incantations to a salve of Dian Cécht, which is used for healing. Dian Cécht was invoked with healing charms into the 8th century CE and even in modern folklore is associated with an herbal oatmeal preparation that has healing properties[7].

The cauldron or well could be used as his symbol, perhaps with herbs in it. Offerings to him might include water, herbal tea, or medicinal herbs.

1. MacKillop, 1998
2. O hOgain, 2006
3. ibid
4. Macalister, 1941
5. MacKillop, 1998
6. O hOgain, 2006
7. MacKillop, 1998

Goibhniu

Goibhniu is the Irish God of smithcraft equated to the Welsh Gafannon. His name is derived from the word for smith; Old Irish gobha, Modern Irish gabha (O hOgain, 2006). According to some folklore Goibhniu needed only three blows from his hammer to forge a weapon[1]. Goibhniu has two brothers, Credne the wright and Luchtne (or Luchtar) the carpenter, forming a trinity of crafting Gods. The three often work together to forge the weapons of the Gods, with each one making a part of the whole. According to the *Lebor Gabala Erenn* (LGE) Dian Cécht was also his brother and they were all sons of Esarg: 'Goibniu and Creidne and Dian Cécht and Luichtne, the four sons of Esarg'[2].

Indeed the four are mentioned together at several points in the LGE such as: 'In his [Nuada's] company were the craftsmen, Goibniu the smith and Creidne the wright and Luichne the carpenter and Dian Cécht the leech.'[3]

Goibniu was the pre-eminent smith of the Tuatha Dé Danann who made weapons in particular. Before the battle of Maige Tuired, Goibniu is asked what he will contribute.

> And he [Lugh] asked his smith, even Goibniu, what power he wielded for them?
>
> 'Not hard to say,' quoth he. 'Though the men of Erin bide in the battle to the end of seven years, for every spear that parts from its shaft, or sword that shall break therein, I will provide a new weapon in its place. No spearpoint which my hand shall forge', saith he, 'shall make a missing cast. No skin which it pierces shall taste life afterwards. That has not been done by Dolb the smith of the Fomorians. I am now [preparing] for the battle of Magh Tuired.'[4]

During the battle against the Fomorians he made peerless spears that never missed and killed whoever they hit, excluding only himself. We learn the latter fact after Brighid's son by Bres, Ruadan, goes to the forge, takes one of Goibhniu's spears and wounds him with it, only to have the smith turn around and kill the would-be assassin with the same spear. Goibhniu is taken to Dian Cécht's healing well and recovers.

The Tuatha Dé Danann received their immortality and perpetual youth from Goibhniu, who had a special drink called the 'fled Goibnenn', which he made for them[5]. Although usually described as an ale or mead, this drink is sometimes also said to be a feast – another meaning of the word fled in Old Irish – and is said by some to cure disease[6]. Besides this special drink, Goibhniu also possessed a magical cow who gave an endless supply of milk[7].

Goibhniu is also invoked in the St Gall's Incantations, giving him a specific association with healing; in this source he is called on to remove a thorn, which may be a metaphor for healing a battle wound: '...rogarg fiss goibnen aird goibnenn renaird goibnenn ceingeth ass'[8] meaning, 'very fierce Goibniu's knowledge, Goibniu's attention, Goibniu's powerful attention overcomes it!' (translation M. Daimler, 2015)

There are also several early Irish charms that invoke that art of Goibhniu for protection[9]. This may be related to the idea that a being who caused an injury or created a weapon had power of the injury itself, something we see in charms relating to the evil eye and elf-shot.

Goibniu is especially associated with Cork, and in particular with Aolbach (Crow Island) on Beara peninsula[10]. He was said to have his forge there and to keep his magic cow in that area. Other folklore associates him with county Cavan and the Iron mountains there[11]. In later Irish mythology Goibniu became Gobhan Saer, a smith and architect of the fairies[12].

A modern pagan might call on Goibniu for anything relating to smithwork or crafting with metal, as well as for healing any injuries from bladed or forged weapons. You could also call on him to bless weapons.

Offerings to him can include weapons, metal, beer, ale, or mead, as well as anything else that feels appropriate. His symbols could be the anvil or smith's hammer.

1. Ellis, 1987
2. Macalister, 1941
3. ibid
4. Stokes, 1926
5. O hOgain, 2006
6. Monaghan, 2004
7. O hOgain, 2006
8. Stokes, 1901

9. O hOgain, 2006
10. ibid
11. Monaghan, 2004
12. Ellis, 1987

Luchta

Also called Luchtain, Luchtaine, Luchtine, or Luchtar. He is the premier carpenter of the Tuatha Dé Danann and with his two brothers, Goibniu and Credne, forms the group that is known as the three Gods of skill. He is particularly known for his skill in making spear shafts and shields[1]. There is little surviving mythology about Luchta and we see him mostly appearing in conjunction with one or more of his brothers, usually preparing for battle by equipping the Gods.

His symbols would include any tools of carpentry or raw materials associated with the craft. Offerings might include milk, ale, or wooden items.

1. MacKillop. 1998

Lugh

One of the most well known of the Irish Gods is Lugh, Lug in Old Irish, who is given several epithets including Lamhfada (long arm), Ildanach (many skilled), and Samildanach (many joined skills). He is also sometimes called either Mac Céin, son of Cian, or Mac Ethlenn, son of Eithne[1]. Lugh was one of the High Kings of the Tuatha Dé Danann, ruling after Nuada, and he was the only one who could defeat his grandfather, the Fomorian Balor, in the second battle of Maige Tuired. During this battle we see Lugh earning his epithet of many-skilled as he earns his way into the High King's hall by proving he has more skills than any other individual member among the Gods and we also see him actively using magical skill to rally his army and to curse the opposing army before battle[2].

Lugh was the son of the Dé Danann Cian and the Fomorian Eithne; his paternal grandfather was the physician God Dian Cécht and his maternal grandfather the dangerous Fomorian Balor who had an evil eye that could kill anyone it looked on. There had been a prophecy that Balor's grandson would kill him so Balor imprisoned his daughter in a tower; Cian snuck in and had a single tryst with Eithne, which resulted in triplets. When Balor found the babies he cast them into the sea where two of them either drown or were turned into seals, while Lugh was saved and fostered by either Manannán or Tailtiu[3]. In *The Ulster Cycle* he is said to be the father of the hero Cu Chulainn by a mortal mother, although Cu Chulainn does simultaneously have a mortal father as well. We see Lugh coming to Cu Chulainn's aid in the *Tain Bo Cuiligne* when the hero is gravely injured, taking him into the Otherworldly sí in order to heal him. In myth and folklore Lugh is given four different wives: Buí (better known as the Cailleach Bhéirre), Nás, Echtach, and Englic[4]. One of these wives was unfaithful and had an affair with the Dagda's son Cermait, prompting Lugh's vengeful killing of him; this in turn eventually led the three sons of Cermait to seek revenge on Lugh for their father's death.

Lugh is most strongly associated with the festival of Lúnasa, which bears his name, although it is more properly understood as a memorial for his foster mother Tailtiu. Lúnasa in old Irish is Lughnasadh, meaning 'funeral assembly of Lugh', while in more modern Irish the name means 'games or assembly of Lugh'. According to the *Lebor Gabala Erenn* Lugh instituted the games of Lúnasa in honor of his foster mother after she died clearing the plain that bore her name[5]. The holiday itself focuses on the celebration of the beginning of the harvest with things like dressing holy wells, horse races, athletic games, and the preparations of special foods. Today many Lúnasa celebrations center on Saint Patrick as a divine protector of the harvest, but it is likely that Lugh originally held this role and was only later replaced when the new religion came in[6].

Lugh may be seen as one of the kings of the Otherworld, particularly associated with Teamhair, as he is depicted as such in the story of Baile in Scáile[7]. He is also strongly associated with the founding of different mortal family lines and several different tribes were named after him[8]. Lugh was the king of the Gods for a time and is portrayed as having a very important role among the others, being both well-known and appearing in a variety of myths. Some scholars suggest that Lugh was an interloper to the Irish pantheon who was only added later and that his mythology reflects this, showing him being born and coming into the crisis between the Tuatha Dé Danann and Fomorians in a way that displaces the existing king Nuada[9]. Whether this is so or not, Lugh was almost certainly a pan-Celtic deity who can be found under similar names in different related cultures. To the Welsh he was Llew Llaw Gyffes, and to the Gaul's he was Lugos; the name is derived from the proto-Indo-European root *leug(h) which most likely means 'to swear an oath'[10].

Lugh possessed one of the four treasures of the Tuatha Dé Danann, said in myth to be either a sword or spear, although it is most often believed to be a spear[11]. In the story Tuath De Danand na Set soim, we are told that this treasure was acquired by Lugh in a city before the Gods came to Ireland, a version echoed in less detail in the Lebor Gabala Erenn, although there is another story about how he gained the spear as well. The Oidheadh Chloinne Tuireann tells us that after Lugh's father Cian was killed by the children of Tuireann, Lugh required them to fulfill a series of impossible tasks and in so doing gained his famous spear. One of the epithets applied to him in the Lebor Gabala Erenn is 'rind-agach', which Macalister gives as 'spear slaughterous'[12] although 'spear-combative' is a closer translation. It is said that whoever had the spear of Lugh could never lose in battle.

Modern pagans may choose to honor Lugh for a variety of reasons since he is associated with such a wide range of skills.

Some of the most common tend to be skill at arms, leadership, and magical skill. Lugh is often honored particularly at Lúnasa, a time when he is said to have contested with Crom for the harvest. Offerings to him could include grain, milk, or the product of any skill that you have put effort into.

1. MacKillop, 1998
2. Gray, 1983
3. MacKillop, 1998
4. ibid
5. MacAlister, 1941
6. MacNeil, 1962
7. Smyth, 1988
8. ibid
9. O hOgain, 2006
10. ibid
11. Daimler, 2015
12. Macalister, 1944

Miach

Miach is the Irish God associated with restoring the lost limb of the High King Nuada. In the *Cath Maige Tuired* we are told that he accomplished the healing of Nuada by carrying the original severed arm against his side for three days, then his chest for three days, then finally for three days he threw bulrushes against it[1]. Afterwards he was given the arm in payment. In the story of Oidheadh Chloinne Tuireann, Miach and his brother Ormiach arrive at Tara where Miach heals the doorkeeper, who has lost an eye, by replacing his missing eye with one from a cat, which has some unfortunate side effects for the doorkeeper[2]. The *Lebor Gabala Erenn* includes several versions of the story of his healing of King Nuada. His father was so jealous of his healing powers that he dealt him four blows, the first three Miach healed, but the fourth killed him; after this every healing herb in the world grew up from his grave and Airmed was organizing them when Dian Cécht scattered them (however, in other versions Miach is not killed)[3]. This is a reflection of the belief that the plants that grow on a person's grave hold some of their spirit, and so what grew from the grave of the healing God were all the healing plants in the world. Of course being a God his death was not permanent, and he appears later in the battle against the Fomorians side by side with his father and siblings healing the wounded of the Tuatha Dé Danann at his father's famous healing well.

His father is the premiere physician God Dian Cécht; he also has several siblings who are associated with healing including his sister Airmed and his brothers Ormiach and Ochtriuil.

Miach can be honored today for any high-tech medical procedures, surgery, or healing over a period of time. Offerings to him might include herb-infused water, herbs associated with healing, or pure water.

1. Gray, 1982
2. ibid
3. Macalister, 1944

Midir

Midir, also known as Midhir, is one of the Tuatha Dé Danann and owner of the sí of Bri Léithe in county Longford. O hOgain suggests the modern Irish for his name would be Mír and posits that it most likely originally meant 'measurer'[1]. An obscure deity, there is not a great deal known about Midir although he features prominently in the story of the Tochmarc Etain. In that story we learn that Midir once lost an eye when he was struck by a holly branch when trying to intervene in a dispute between Oengus and Elcmar, but that Dian Cécht healed the wound and restored the eye[2]. He is associated with cranes and swans and was known to transform into the shape of a swan in at least one story[3].

Midir is one of the foster parents of the Dagda's son Oengus mac Og, and various sources list him as either the brother or father of the Dagda. He had two wives, the sorceress Fuamnach and the king's daughter Etain; the rivalry of these two women forms the basis of the story of the Tochmarc Etain. He has two daughters, Ailbe and Doirind[4].

The most well-known place associated with him is Brí Leith (gray hill) in county Longford.

Some modern practitioners relate Midir to the moon, although this connection is uncertain. He could also be seen as a God of compromises, negotiations, balance, and commitment. Offerings to him might include milk, water, or fresh herbs.

1. O hOgain, 2006
2. Leahy, 1906
3. Smyth, 1988
4. MacKillop, 1998

Nechtan

Also called Neachtan, he was the possessor or guardian of Connla's Well, a sacred well of wisdom that only he and his three cupbearers were allowed to pull water from. Some modern scholars believe that Nechtan is another name for Nuada Airgetlam, as both may have older roots as Gods associated with water cults[1]. Nechtan is generally considered a God related to rivers and water[2].

Nechtan's wife was the river Goddess Boann, also said to be the wife of Elcmar, leading some to also suggest that Nechtan and Elcmar are the same personage. By this logic one might argue that Nechtan, Elcmar, and Nuada are all names for a single deity. Carberry Hill in Kildare is said to be the sí of Nechtan[3].

1. MacKillop, 1998
2. Sjoestedt, 2000
3. MacKillop, 1998

Nuada Airgetlamh

Nuada was the king of the Tuatha Dé Danann when they first came to Ireland; in the *Lebor Gabala Erenn* it is said that he ruled for seven years before the Tuatha Dé came to Ireland, was displaced when he lost an arm in battle, and then ruled a further 20 years after being healed[1]. Green suggests that Nuada's name may mean 'cloud-maker' and suggests that his counterparts in other cultures include the Gaulish Nodens, Welsh Nudd/Ludd, and possibly the Germanic Tyr[2]. The arguments put forth to connect the deities etymologically are reasonably sound, relying on the shared reconstructed Indo-European roots of 'noudont' or 'noudent', which means 'to catch' and proto-Indo-European root 'neu-d', which means 'to acquire' or 'to utilize'[3]. However, as with anything involving reconstructed language, it is still only theoretical. There also seems to be a fairly strong mythological connection between these deities, particularly around the loss of an arm and replacement of the limb with one of silver. O hOgain suggests that Nuada's name may mean 'catcher' and theorizes that Nuada is the same deity as Nechtan and Elcmar[4]. He suggests this based on another name for Nuada being Nuada Necht, which O hOgain believes is the earlier form of Nechtan; by this association Nuada would have been the original owner of Brugh na Boyne and would also possess the source of the Boyne, the well of Nechtan. Although difficult to prove with certainty, this would reflect the strong connection to water seen in the related British deity, Nodens. Other sources also suggest Nuada being the same deity as Nechtan and Elcmar, making him the husband of Boand who is cuckolded by the Dagda and then tricked out of possession of the Brugh na Boyne by Boand and Dagda's son from the affair, Oengus[5].

Nuada's most well-known epithet is Airgetlamh, silver hand or arm. His name also appears as Nuadha, Nuadae, Nuadai, and Nuodai, with alternate spellings of his epithet as Aircetlaum[6]. In the story of the *Cath Maige Tuired*, Nuada was said to have lost his arm in battle, after which Dian Cécht, with the help of the smith Credne, fashioned him a new arm of silver that looked and moved just as a real arm would[7]. According to a note by Gray in the Index to Persons of the *Cath Maige Tuired* there is a story where Nuada's severed arm is carried off after the battle by a hawk[8]. Because of this disfigurement Nuada was forced to forfeit his kingship, for the law of the Tuatha Dé stated that only an unblemished king could rule[9]. O hOgain suggests, in his book *The Lore of Ireland*, that the original story of the loss of Nuada's arm may have actually involved an accident with his own sword, or even an intentional sacrifice, and that there may have been some connection to healing waters or even that his lost arm may have been symbolic of a river[10]. During the medieval period the story was expanded to include more details; it was his right arm that was lost in battle with the Fir Bolg warrior Streang[11]. Nuada was carried from the field only to return the next day with the request that Streang tie his own right arm to ensure fair combat – when Streang refused, the other Tuatha Dé Danann offered a province of land to keep Nuada from risking his life in an unequal fight[12]. At this point Bres became king, but after seven years Dian Cécht fashioned the silver arm, then his son Miach, possibly along with his brother Ormiach, replaced it with an arm of flesh and Nuada took back the kingship beginning the second battle of Maige Tuired[13]. During the second battle Nuada gave the kingship to Lugh, who organized the battle and fought the fearsome Fomorian Balor, who is Lugh's grandfather[14]. By some accounts Nuada ruled for 20 years after being healed, while others state that he and Macha died together in the second battle of Maige Tuired at the hand of Balor the Fomorian king[15].

Nuada was the son of Echtach, and had four sons Tadg, Caither, Cucharn, and Etaram the poet, as well as a daughter Echtge; no mother is mentioned[16]. He is said in some sources to be married to Macha, one of the three Morrignae, and he possessed one of the four treasures brought to Ireland by the

Tuatha Dé, a sword which once unsheathed no enemy could escape and no wound from it could be healed[17].

If one believes that Nuada was the original owner of the Brugh na Boyne it would appear that after losing the Brugh to Angus, Nuada moved to Sí Chleitigh, although alternate stories later claim his home to be Sí Almhu or Slievenamon[18].

Nuada is a God of war, battle, justice, leadership, hunting, and if we agree with his connection to Nechtan and Elcmar we can also see him as a deity of healing and rivers[19]. Modern practitioners could associate hawks, dogs, or salmon with him, and the sword is often seen as his symbol because he possessed the sword which was one of the four treasures. Offerings to Nuada might include fish, beer, or Guinness.

1. Macalister, 1941
2. Green, 1992
3. Nodens, 2012
4. O hOgain, 2006
5. Monaghan, 2004
6. Gray, 1983
7. Macalister, 1941
8. Gray, 1983
9. Monaghan, 2004; Macalister, 1941
10. O hOgain, 2006
11. O hOgain, 2006; Gray, 1983
12. ibid
13. Macalister, 1941; Monaghan, 2004; O hOgain, 2006
14. Green, 1992
15. Gray, 1983; Macalister, 1941
16. Gray, 1983
17. Berresford Ellis, 1987, O hOgain, 2006; Jones, 2012
18. Green, 1992; Monaghan, 2004; O hOgain, 2006
19. Gray, 1983; Jones, 2012

Ogma

Ogma, also spelled Oghma, his epithets are Grianeces (sun poet) and Grianainech (sun faced)[1]. He is both a famed warrior and known for his eloquence; he, the Dagda, and Lugh are often listed as the three champions of the Tuatha Dé Danann[2]. When Lugh first arrives at the hall of the High King in the story of the *Cath Maige Tuired* Ogma challenges him to a test of strength, which Lugh wins. During that same story when asked what he will contribute to the battle, Ogma promises to defeat kings along with a significant portion of the opposing army, and in the final battle he takes on one of the main Fomorian kings in combat.

Ogma's father is Elatha, his brothers are the Dagda, Bres, Delbaeth, and Eloth. His brother Bres is not the same Bres is the half-Fomorian High King of the Tuatha Dé Danann, but a different similarly named person, just as Ogma's brother Delbaeth shouldn't be confused with his similarly named son. His wife is Etan, a poet and daughter of Dian Cécht, and his sons are Tuireann, Delbaeth, and the poet Cairpre[3].

Ogma is the creator, in myth, of the Ogham alphabet, which bears his name. It's said that he created the Ogham to prove his own ingenuity as a God of skill and eloquence[4]. He also possesses a sword named Orna which, when drawn from its sheath, tells everything it has done[5]. Ogma is known as both a great warrior and also as a God of poetic skill and verbal eloquence.

Modern practitioners may choose to honor him for either his physical prowess, his ability with words, or both. As a God connected to poets, one could choose to see the harp as his symbol, and since two of his epithets relate to the sun, one might also use that as his symbol. Honey would be a good offering to him as would mead.

1. MacKillop, 1998; O hOgain, 2006
2. Smyth, 1988

3. Macalister, 1944
4. Calder, 1917
5. Sjoestedt, 2000

Chapter 2

Tuatha Dé Danann: Goddesses

Áine

Her name, which is the same in both Old Irish and modern Irish, likely means 'brightness' or 'splendor' and she is often associated with the sun[1]. She is known to us from mythology as one of the Tuatha Dé Danann, but also in folklore as a Queen of Fairy who was honored even into the last century. Áine's epithet is 'na gClair' (of the Wisps) and she is also sometimes called Áine Chlair, a word that may relate to wisps or may be an old name for the Kerry or Limerick area[2].

She is said in some sources to be the daughter of Manannán Mac Lir and in others to be the daughter of Manannán's foster son Eogabail, a Druid of the Tuatha Dé Danann[3]. No mother is listed for her, nor even hinted at in mythology. In other sources she is said to be the daughter of Fer I (Yew Man) and the wife or lover of Manannán; in either case she remains connected to Manannán one way or another in every version[4]. She may have two sisters; one is Grian (literally 'sun') and the other is Finnen, whose name means white[5].

Áine is well known in later folklore for her love affairs with human men and several Irish families claim to be her descendants. The most well known of these human descendants are the Fitzgeralds, who trace their ancestry from the third Earl of Desmond, Gearoid Iarla, the son of Áine and the second Earl of Desmond. It is said by some that Gearoid did not die, but was taken into Loch Guir and would return one day, and they also say that he appears every seven years and rides around the loch on a white horse[6]. Other tales say that he lives still within the lake and can be seen riding beneath the water on a white fairy horse, while still other stories claim that Áine turned him into a goose on the shore of the lake[7]. In another story, the story of the Cath Maige Mucrama, Áine was also said to have been raped by King Aillil Olom, on Samhain, who stories say she either bit off the ear from or she killed in punishment[8]. The child of this union was Eogan whose line went on to claim rulership of the land through their descent from the Goddess; the Eóganacht are another family then who claim descent from Áine through this connection[9].

Through her stories Áine is associated with fertility, agriculture, sovereignty, and the sun, as well as love. She is associated especially with red mares, with some people claiming she could assume this form[10]. She may also be associated more generally with horses, and possibly with geese and sheep as they appear in her folklore.

The hill of Cnoc Áine in Limerick is one of the most well known places associated with her, said to have been named after her during the settling of Ireland when she used magic to help her father win the area[11]. Additionally there is another hill called Cnoc Áine in county Derry, and a third in Donegal[12]. In Ulster there is a well called Tobar Áine that bears her name. Not far from Áine's hill is another hill, Cnoc Gréine, associated with the Goddess Grian; some sources list the two as sisters and a few scholars suggest that the two might symbolize the summer and winter suns[13].

Midsummer was her special holy day and up until the 19th century people continued to celebrate her on the eve of Midsummer with a procession around the hill, carrying torches of burning straw in honor of Áine na gClair[14]. On Midsummer, clumps of straw would be lit on her hill and then scattered through the cultivated fields and cows to propitiate Áine's blessing[15]. In county Louth there is a place called Dun Áine where people believe that the weekend after Lughnasa belongs to Áine, and in some folklore she is said to be the consort of Crom Cruach during the three days of Lughnasa[16].

In modern contexts Áine is often looked to as a Goddess of

love, fertility, abundance, and sovereignty. Offerings to her may include any agricultural produce, especially those you grow yourself, milk, cream, or baked goods.

1. O hOgain, 2006; Monaghan, 2004
2. ibid
3. Ellis, 1987
4. MacKillop, 1998
5. Monaghan, 2004
6. Ellis, 1987; MacKillop, 1998
7. Ellis, 1987
8. Monaghan, 2004; Berresford Ellis, 1987; O hOgain, 2006
9. MacKillop, 1998; Monaghan, 2004
10. ibid
11. O hOgain, 2006
12. ibid
13. MacKillop, 1998; Monaghan, 2004
14. Ellis, 1987
15. O hOgain, 2006
16. O hOgain, 2006; MacNeill, 1962

Airmed

Airmed or Airmid in Old Irish, and Airmeith and Airmedh in modern Irish, her name is from the word airmed, which means a dry measure or measure of grain[1]. She is associated with healing in general and herbal healing in particular.

She is the daughter of the healing God Dian Cécht and sister of Miach, Ormiach, Ochtriuil, Cu, Cethan, and Cian, and she has at least one sister, the poet Etan. No mother is mentioned for her in mythology.

In the story of the healing of King Nuada by Miach, after Miach died Airmed found healing herbs growing from his grave and harvested them; she laid all the herbs out on her cloak and organized them to preserve the knowledge of their properties[2].

According to the story the herbs numbered 365, with one for each of his sinews and joints, and one for every possible bodily ailment, but when Dian Cécht saw the way she had laid them out he scattered them. Later in the same tale, the *Cath Maige Tuired*, we find Airmed with her father and two of her brothers, Octriuil and Miach, at her father's healing well helping to heal the injured warriors of the Tuatha Dé Danann.

Many people today associate her especially with herbal healing. I have often used a mortar and pestle to represent her on my altar; she is also associated with the cloak or mantle, called a brat in Irish. Offerings to her could include herbs, water, or milk.

1. MacKillop, 1998; eDIL, n.d.
2. Gray, 1983

Anu

Anu's name appears in the older myths as Anand or Anann. Her name has a meaning related to wealth or abundance. She is associated with Munster in particular and with two hills in County Kerry called the Dá Chich Anann (two breasts of Anu). She is often conflated with or assumed to be identical to Danu, but there is as much evidence to contradict that idea as to support it.

In the *Lebor Gabala Erenn* we are told that Anand is the personal name of the Morrigan: 'Ernmas had three other daughters, Badb and Macha and Morrigu, whose name was Anand'[1]. Much like the confusion with Danu, it's uncertain if this can be entirely trusted though. It is possible that Anu is the same as Danu and also the Morrigan, but she may also be a unique deity in herself.

Ultimately, Anu is an obscure figure and different people, including academics, have reached their own conclusions about who she is. Many modern pagans see her as a kind of earth mother or divine mother figure, while some see her as a sovereignty figure. Those who wish to connect to her have little mythology to work with so the alternative is meditation and personal experiences. Offerings to her would be left to the individual to decide.

1. Macalister, 1944

Badb

Badhbh, whose name is more familiar to people in the Old Irish form of Badb, is a Goddess who is known as both an individual being and as one of the Morrigans. Her name has a variety of meanings including a hooded crow, venomous, warlike, dangerous, and deadly[1]. The hooded crow is one of the forms that Badb is known to shapeshift into, as are Macha and the Morrigan, and both crows and ravens are associated with her. Her epithet is Badb Catha, literally 'battle crow'. The word badb (lower case b) is also sometimes translated as witch, although it can be used to describe any kind of supernatural woman.

Badb is the daughter of Ernmas and Delbaeth and has several sisters including Macha, the Morrigan, Eriu, Fodla, and Banba; she has two children Ferr Doman and Fiamain[2]. In the *Banshenchus* she is said to be the wife of the Dagda, but in the *Lebor Gabala Erenn* we are told she is one of the two wives of the war God Neit. In mythology she often appears in a grouping of three either with Macha and the Morrigan or with Nemain and 'Be Neit', an obscure figure whose name either means 'wife of Neit' or 'woman of battle'.

In *The Ulster Cycle* Badb appears as a force of incitement, often encouraging Cu Chulainn to fight, and in some versions of the story of Cu Chulainn's death she appears as a crow who flies over him and lands on the pillar he has tied himself to as signal that he has died[3]. Her cries are said to cause panic, chaos, and confusion among warriors, which is how she affects battles. She can incite warriors to heroic frenzy or terrify them into panicked collapse by shrieking and it is even said that in one 9th century battle she appeared and incited the armies to slaughter each other[4]. In the first battle of Maige Tuired the Fomorian poet, seeing the terrible slaughter of both armies, declares that 'The red Badb will thank them for the battle-combats'[5]. This reinforces a common theme with Badb, that like the carrion crows and ravens she enjoys aftermath of war. The Red Badb or Red Mouthed Badb is a common name for her.

Besides death and battle, Badb is associated with prophecy. After the final battle with the Fomorians a great prophecy is given and we are told that Badb relates all such news. Before Cu Chulainn goes to his final battle he sees an ill omen, a woman washing his bloody armor and weeping, which is sometimes is said to be Badb, or her unnamed daughter[6]. In later folklore she appears as the washer-at-the-ford, presaging the deaths of those who see her by washing their clothes or armor; she is believed to be the source of the later bean sí (banshee) figure[7].

Badb is a complex deity associated with prophecy, battle, death, madness, and magic. Modern practitioners may seek her out for her wisdom and her ability to relieve the same things she causes. She is particularly connected to crows and ravens, as well as the colors black, white, and red. Offerings to her may include whiskey, rum, blood, water, or milk, and some of her followers choose to feed the birds associated with her as an offering to her.

1. eDIL, n.d.
2. Macalister, 1941; Gray, 1983
3. Smyth, 1988; Green, 1992
4. Green, 1992; O hOgain, 2006
5. Frazer, 1916
6. O hOgain, 2006
7. Green, 1992

Banba

Her name was Banbha in Old Irish and means 'place of women's death'[1]. Banba was one of the primary land and sovereignty Goddesses of Ireland as a whole and her name is still used as an alternate name for Ireland by poets.

Banba is the daughter of Eirnin, according to one source, and the daughter of Ernmas according to another and her two sisters are Eriu and Fotla; she is said to be the wife of Etar (great) and Mac Coll (son of Hazel)[2]. Just as her mother is disputed so is her father, with some sources saying she is the daughter of Delbeath and others that her father is Cian or Fiachra[3]. The *Lebor Gabala Erenn* says that her sisters also include the Morrigan, Badb, and Macha, while the *Foras Feasa ar Éirinn* says that Banba, Eriu, and Fotla worshipped the Morrigan, Badb, and Macha as deities[4]. Her daughter is Cessair one of the first settlers of Ireland, although in an 8th century text it was Banba herself who originally was the first settler of Ireland along with 150 of her followers; only later was this changed and her role taken over by her daughter[5]. O hOgain mentions that according to some stories Banba survived the biblical flooding of the world by staying in a place in Ireland that was never covered by water, making her the first and oldest continuous inhabitant of the island.

The *Banshenchus* describes her as 'ardent'[6]. In the story of the arrival of the Gaels to Ireland, the children of Mil meet Banba as they are first traveling the land and she asks them to promise that Ireland will always bear her name, linking her to the sovereignty of the island. It is likely, however, that she was originally a sovereignty Goddess of south Leinster and Meath in particular, and she was strongly associated with Tara[7].

Those seeking to connect to Ireland as a whole or to its culture may choose to honor Banba, or the trio of Banba and her sisters together. Offerings to her may include traditional poetry, music, or artwork that honors Irish culture as well as the usual milk or grain.

1. O hOgain, 2006
2. MacKillop, 1998; MacAlister, 1944
3. MacKillop, 1998; *Banshenchus*, n.d.
4. Macalister, 1944; Keating, 1857
5. O hOgain, 2006
6. *Banshenchus*, n.d.
7. MacKillop, 1998; O hOgain, 2006

Bóinn

Bóinn in modern Irish is Boand or Boann in Old Irish; her name is likely derived from Bo-fhionn meaning 'white cow'. When she appears in myth she is usually referred to as 'the Bóinn' just as the Dagda or the Morrigan are always referred to with the definitive article before their names. She appears at some length in the story of Aislinge Oenguso, where we see her always referred to this way, and where she acts to help her son when he needs advice and support.

The river Boyne is named for this Goddess and she has strong ties to Brugh na Boinne and the Newgrange complex. She is also strongly associated with poetry and in some early literature it was said that to drink from her river in June would grant the gifts of both poetry and seership[1]. In one version of the story that tells how the river Boyne came to exist we learn that Bóinn went to Nechtan's Well, which only he and his cupbearers were allowed to access, and when she approached the water surged up three times, injuring her leg, arm, and eye; she tried to flee, but the water followed her, creating the river[2]. In another similar version it was the Well of Segais that she offended and that rose up and chased her to create the river[3]. The cow is the main animal associated with her, particularly white cows. Daragh Smyth suggests that her association with cattle is representative of the phases of the moon, with white, red, brown, and dark cows representing each phase from full to dark[4].

In mythology the Bóinn is said to be the wife of Nechtan or

Elcmar, who may be the same personage, and who each may be alternate names for Nuada[5]. She was also well known for having an affair with the Dagda, with whom she produced a child, Aengus, who was conceived and born on the same day through the Dagda's magic to prevent her husband from finding out about their affair. No other children are known to be hers although some people speculate that the Dagda's daughter Brighid may also be Bóinn's.

Modern practitioners may choose to associate her with poetry, prophecy, and abundance. She could be prayed to or invoked for any of these things, or for anything else connected to her in mythology. Offerings to her could include milk, cream, butter, or clear water.

1. O hOgain, 2006
2. ibid
3. MacKillop, 1998
4. Smyth, 1988
5. O hOgain, 2006

Brighid

There are many versions of Brighid's name, both ancient and modern. She is called Brighid, Brigid, Brigit, or Bríd, and in Old Irish her name may appear as Brig or Bric. Her name in Old Irish, Brig, has a variety of meanings including authority, strength, vigor, and power[1]. Brighid is a complicated deity who is seen as both an individual and three sisters who share the same name; she is usually associated with poetry, smithcraft, and healing. O hOgain says that Brighid is a protector and inspirer of poets, as well as being connected to agricultural fertility. The 9th century glossaries say that 'among all the Irish a Goddess used to be called a Brigit'[2]. Many, if not all, Irish deity names are actually titles or epithet so it's difficult to be certain how meaningful that entry was or if it is indicative of a belief in the earlier pagan period, but it is a statement about Brighid's significance.

Brighid is the daughter of the Dagda and an unnamed mother; through her father she has multiple siblings including Aengus mac Og, Cearmait, Aodh Caomh, Conan, Midir, Bodhbh Dearg, and Ainge[3]. In some versions of the *Lebor Gabala Erenn* she is given as the mother of the three Gods of Danu, which is where some people come to think that she may be the same deity as Danu, although it is impossible to know with certainty if this is so, or only a medieval attempt to reconcile the pagan mythology into a more cohesive system. In mythology she has a son Ruadan with the half-Fomorian, half-Dé Danann King Bres; in some stories she also had three sons with Tuireann named Brian, Iachar, and Iucharba although in other versions they are the sons of Danu, or are sons of Bres possibly with Brighid[4]. She may be the grandmother of Ecne, who represents wisdom, knowledge, and enlightenment[5].

In later periods Brighid was syncretized with the Catholic Saint Brigid making it hard in many places to distinguish the mythology of one from the other. The information we have relating to Brighid comes from the traditional mythology including the *Cath Maige Tuired* and *Lebor Gabala Erenn* as well as mythology of the Christian saint of the same name who many believe is a continuation of the Goddess. Different authors disagree on how much and what should be attributed to the Goddess or the saint, but we can at least say that the material clearly attributed to Brighid of the Tuatha Dé Danann belongs to the Goddess.

Imbolc is a holy day dedicated to Brighid, celebrated on February 1st or 2nd, although Alexander Carmichael in *The Carmina Gadelica* mentions an older date as well, of February 13th. This reflects the tradition prior to the shifting of the calendar from Julian to Gregorian, which moved all the dates back by about two weeks. *The Carmina Gadelica* mentions several traditions relating to this holiday, particularly relating to welcoming

Brighid into the home, purifying the house, blessing it and making protective talismans. There are some modern stories that connect Brighid and the Cailleach at Imbolc; some people say that Imbolc is the day that the Cailleach Bhur releases Brighid who has been held prisoner all winter, while others say that Aengus rescues his sister. Still another version says that Brighid and the Cailleach are the same deity, and that at Samhain Brighid becomes the Cailleach while at Imbolc she drinks form a sacred spring that turns her back into Brighid. Although the ideas connecting Brighid and the Cailleach are entirely modern, dating no further back than the 20th century, they have become increasingly popular among neopagans.

Brighid was said to have several animals who were kings of their respective species including a ram as well as two oxen and a pig who would cry out 'after rapine had been committed in Ireland'[6]. This likely reflects her connection to both domestic animals and through them symbolically to different strata of society, including women, farmers, and warriors. O hOgain sees her as a mother Goddess, relating Saint Brigid's role as foster mother to Christ to the pagan Goddess's role as a mother deity responsive to her followers. Brighid has associations with grief and mourning as well, as in myth she is the first person to ever caoine (keen) or cry out in mourning when her son Ruadán is killed[7].

Brighid has a many healing wells in Ireland, including wells in almost every county, but her most well-known site is at Kildare near the Black Abbey. These wells are associated with water that has healing powers and Brighid also has a talisman called a brat Bhríde (Brigid's mantle or cloak), which is a small piece of cloth left out on Imbolc eve to be blessed by the Goddess/saint, which would then have healing properties throughout the year. She is the tutelary Goddess of Leinster, and besides her association with Kildare she is also likely connected to Corleck Hill in county Cavan[8]. According to Carmichael her special bird is the oystercatcher, which in Scottish is named Bridein, Bride's bird, and Gille Bride, page of Bride. The linnet is also special to the Goddess and is named bigein Bride, little bird of Bride. Brighid's flower is said to be the dandelion.

Brighid is usually associated with poetry, healing, smithcraft, fertility, livestock, motherhood, fire, water, and by some people also with grief. Offerings to Brighid could include milk, butter, cheese, and bread, and traditionally might sometimes include chickens. For a modern practitioner these would all still be viable options and reflect Brighid's connection to agriculture and dairy products.

1. eDIL, n.d.
2. O hOgain, 2006
3. ibid
4. Daimler, 2016
5. MacKillop, 1998
6. Macalister, 1944
7. O hOgain, 2006
8. MacKillop, 1998

Cliodhna

Cliodhna, also known as Clíona, is considered both one of the Tuatha Dé Danann in older mythology and a Fairy Queen in modern folk lore. Her name may mean 'the territorial one', likely reflecting her earlier role as a sovereignty Goddess; her epithet is Ceannfhionn (fair headed or fair haired) and she is sometimes called 'the shapely one'[1]. In many stories she is described as exceptionally beautiful.

Her sister is said to be Aibheall, and her father is Gebann, the Druid of Manannán mac Lir[2]. There are no references to who her mother might be or to her children among the Gods. Several mortal families trace their descent from her including the McCarthys and O'Keefes and she was well known for taking mortal lovers.

Cliodhna is said to have taken the form of a wren, a bird that may be associated with her, and she is also often associated with the Otherworldly Bean sidhe. By some accounts she herself is considered to be such a spirit, or their queen, although in other folklore she is more generally the queen of the fairies of Munster. She has three magical birds that eat Otherworldly apples and have the power to lull people to sleep by singing and then heal them[3].

She is strongly associated with the shore and with waves, and the tide at Glandore in Cork was called the 'Wave of Cliodhna'[4]. In several of her stories she is drowned at that same location after leaving the Otherworld either to try to woo Aengus or after running away with a warrior named Ciabhán. She has a reputation in many stories for her passionate nature and love of poets in particular, and in later folklore when she is considered a Fairy Queen she is known to abduct handsome young poets or to appear and try to seduce them. In folklore she has a reputation for seducing and drowning young men[5].

Cliodhna is particularly associated with the province of Munster and especially with Cork, where she resides at a place called Carraig Chlíona (Cliodhna's rock)[6]. It is likely that she was originally one of the sovereignty Goddesses of Munster and that her survival in folklore to the present period reflects how deeply ingrained she was in local lore.

Modern practitioners may choose to honor Cliodhna for her role as a sovereignty Goddess or as an ancestral deity related to specific families. I might suggest, given her more recent folklore related to the Bean sidhe and her penchant in stories for harming young men and poets, that she should be approached with caution. Offerings to her could include the traditional milk or bread given to the Gods and fairies, as well as poetry, of which she seems fond.

1. O hOgain, 2006; MacKillop, 1998
2. Smyth, 1988; MacKillop, 1998
3. ibid
4. O hOgain, 2006
5. Smyth, 1988
6. O hOgain, 2006

Danu

Although known in modern Irish as Danu her name appears only in the genitive form of Danann or Danand (or similar variants) in Old Irish.

Her parentage is uncertain, but in some myths she is said to be the daughter of Delbeath and Ernmas and by some accounts to be the mother of the three sons of Delbeath as well, although the latter is contradicted in different sources[1]. In the *Cath Maige Tuired Cunga* she is referred to as the foster mother of the Morrigan, Macha, and Badb[2]. She is almost ubiquitously referred to as the mother of the Gods because of the usual translation of 'Tuatha Dé Danann' as 'people of the Goddess Danu'.

Danu is described as being both one of the witches of the Irish Gods as well as one of the female Druids among them[3]. In the first battle of Maige Tuired, Danu accompanies the warriors into the battle along with Macha, Badb, and the Morrigan in one instance and again later with the addition of Bechuille; on the second occasion the story tells us that the five Goddesses fix pillars into the ground so that none could flee the battlefield[4].

There are no surviving ancient myths about Danu, but several modern authors including Peter Berresford Ellis and Alexei Kondratiev have written versions of a Celtic creation story that features her. Two hills in Kerry are named for her, called the 'Two Breasts of Danu'[5].

Many modern Irish pagans see Danu as a mother and land Goddess and connect to her in these ways. She is often honored as a primal mother, or progenitor of all life, and I have seen her take on the role of an Irish version of the Greek Gaia.

1. Keating, 1857; Macalister, 1944
2. Frazer, 1916
3. Keating, 1857; Macalister, 1944
4. Frazer, 1916
5. Keating, 1857

Eriu

Eriu's name may be derived from an earlier Celtic word for 'land' and certainly her name came to be used synonymously for Ireland itself[1].

Eriu's husband was the king Mac Gréine (literally Son of the Sun) and the *Banshenchus* calls her the consort of Cetar (possibly meaning First) who may or may not be another name for Mac Gréine[2]. She is also the lover of the Fomorian King Elatha, and by him the mother of Eochaid Bres[3]. Her father is usually given as Delbeath and her mother as either Ernmas or Einin; her foster father is named Codal[4]. As the tutelary Goddess of Ireland itself it is possible that when sovereignty is personified in stories and not specifically named it is Eriu. MacKillop suggest as much in his *Dictionary of Celtic Mythology*, where he posits that Eriu also appears as Lugh's consort in the story of Baile in Scáil although she is never named.

Eriu's domain was Uisneach in Meath, an important ritual centre of pagan Ireland[5]. In her most well known myth she met the Gaels when they were invading Ireland and told them she would bless their venture if they would promise that Ireland would always bear her name; the Druid Amergin White-knee swore that it would be so and the Milesians were successful in conquering the island. Eriu is described as wearing circlets and ring designs, and although she is often described as a land Goddess the circle imagery along with her pairing to Mac Gréine causes some scholars to suggest that she is a solar or lunar deity[6].

The *Banshenchus* calls her 'fierce' and says that she and her two sisters were 'spirited of speech'[7]. In the story where she meets the Gaels she is quick to respond to an insult from the Milesian Donn by foretelling – or promising – his death and that none of his descendants will live in Ireland because he has offended her. She is often and repeatedly associated with different divine kings, reinforcing her role as a Goddess of sovereignty.

Modern pagans who seek to connect to Ireland itself, particularly the land in its entirety, may wish to connect to or honor Eriu. Offerings to her can include any offerings traditional for the Gods, such as milk or butter.

1. O hOgain, 2006
2. *Banshenchus*, n.d.; Smyth, 1988
3. Gray, 1983
4. MacKillop, 1998
5. O hOgain, 2006
6. Smyth, 1988; MacKillop, 1998
7. *Banshenchus*, n.d.

Etain

In modern Irish her name may appear as Eadaoin; in Old Irish it appears in a wide array of forms including Etaoin, Étaein, Ettain, Etaine, Etáiniu, Etáini, Étaíne, Edaine. The most widely recognized form is probably Etain. The etymology of her name is not entirely certain, but is believed to be based on the word ét (envy) and is usually understood to mean 'one who provokes envy'[1]. Etain is widely regarded in mythology as incomparably beautiful and is referred to as the most beautiful woman in Ireland. Dáithí O hOgain gives her epithet in her most well-known myth as 'Eachraidhe' (Old Irish Echraide), a term in Old Irish for horses, usually used to refer to paired chariot horses.

Etain's parentage is complex because she is said to have been born twice. The first time she is the daughter of a king named Ailill; the second time she is born to a mortal woman named Etar and her husband, who was a champion. Her husbands are first the God Midhir and then, in her second incarnation, the human king named Eochaid, before becoming Midhir's wife again[2]. She has a daughter, Esa, by Eochaid, and another (or possibly the same by another name) called Etain Og, or Etain the Young[3]. She is not known to have had any siblings, but Aengus mac Og was her good friend.

Etain's best preserved myth is the Tochmarc Etaine, which tells the story of how she came to marry Midhir through Aengus's intervention. She goes to live with her new husband, but his first wife, the sorceress Fuamnach (Noisy One) is jealous of his affection for Etain and uses her magic to turn her rival into a puddle of water. Etain subsequently turns into a worm and then a purple fly, but Midhir still loves her all the same so Fuamnach conjures a wind to blow the fly away. After being battered by this wind for years Etain is finally found by Aengus who shelters her in his home at Brugh na Boyne. Eventually Fuamnach finds out she is there and finds a way to distract Aengus, once more using the magical wind to drive Etain off. This time Etain ends up falling into the cup of a human woman, Etar, who becomes pregnant and gives birth to Etain. When she grows up a second time she marries a human king, but her divine husband Midhir tracks her down and seeks to win her back and remind her of her true nature. He eventually prevails and he and Etain return to his home in the form of swans[4].

Her mythic motifs connect her to sovereignty and her horse-related epithet may connect her to other Celtic Goddesses such as Rhiannon and Epona[5]. The Banshenchus calls Etain 'impetuous and swift' and lists her with the magic users of the Tuatha Dé Danann[6].

Modern practitioners may choose to relate to her in a variety of ways. Her mythology may lend itself to understanding her as a Goddess of difficult choices, enduring hardships, and personal power in adversity. She could be associated with winged insects, possible butterflies, horses, and swans, as well as the color purple. Offerings to Etain might include fresh flowers or herbs, or clear water.

1. O hOgain, 2006
2. O hOgain, 2006
3. MacKillop, 1998
4. Daimler, 2015
5. MacKillop, 1998
6. *Banshenchus*, n.d.

Fand

Fand's name may mean either 'tear', from fand, or 'weak; soft', from fann; the etymology is uncertain[1].

Her mother is Flidais, and in some sources her father is named as Aed; her sister is Lí Ban[2]. She is the wife of the sea God Manannán and the lover of the epic hero Cú Chulainn.

Fand's most famous myth is the Serglige Con Culainn, which tells the story of Fand and her sister, Lí Ban, appearing to Cú Chulainn in a dream, where they beat him with whips. After waking Cú Chulainn falls into a sickness until Lí Ban comes to him and tells him that Fand has fallen in love with him; he and Fand become lovers for a period of time until Cú Chulainn's wife intervenes and fights to regain her husband. Eventually Manannán intercedes and uses his magical cloak to make Fand and Cú Chulainn forget each other so that they can return to their respective lives.

Modern practitioners may seek to connect to Fand as Goddess of the ocean because of her role as wife of Manannán or may relate to her as a Goddess of love. Offerings to her could include milk, honey, or bread.

1. MacKillop, 1998; eDIL, n.d.
2. MacKillop, 1998

Flidais

Called Fliodhais in modern Irish and Flidais in Old Irish, her name may mean 'wet one'; she is especially associated with milk and milking[1]. Her epithet is foltchaoin meaning 'soft haired'. Monaghan suggests that her name means 'doe' and sees parallels between Flidias and continental Goddesses such as Arto, Artemis, and Diana[2].

Her husband was Adammair in one source and her son Nia Segamain[3]. In the *Lebor Gabala Erenn* her children are listed as Arden, Be Chuille, Dinand, and Be Teite and the *Metrical Dindeshenchas* list her as the mother of Fand[4]. By this count she was a prolific mother, with a total of five daughters and one son that we know of. In the Driving of the Cattle of Flidais she appears as a mortal character, the lover of Fergus mac Rog and wife of Ailill Finn[5]. So powerful a lover was Flidais that even though Fergus normally needed seven women to satisfy him, when he was with Flidais she alone could do it.

Flidais is the owner of magical cattle, both a cow that gives copious amounts of milk and wild deer that were her cattle; two of her daughters, Be Chuille and Dinand, are called 'she-farmers' connecting them to the produce of the earth, with another, Nia Segamain, mentioned in relation to her cattle[6]. She also has a herd of deer that gave milk like cows, and her herds are made up of both deer and cows[7]. She is associated with both domestic cattle and deer, and all animals are said to be her 'cattle'[8]. Several of her myths feature her feeding large numbers of people with the bounty from her magical herds: during the *Tain Bo Cuiligne* she supplied milk from her herd once a week that fed the whole army of Connacht, and in the Driving of the Herd of Flidais her single magical cow fed 300 men at each milking[9].

Not all of Flidais's qualities are entirely positive. In the

Banshenchus we are told that she is connected to fighting and the destruction of men. It says: 'Flidais... Though slender she destroyed young men. She decreed hard close fighting.'[10]. Although this is the only such reference, she is the source of the conflict in the Driving of the Herd of Flidais so perhaps this reflects an aspect of her that can incite violence.

Modern Irish pagans often associate Flidais with the woodlands and with wild animals, although in mythology she is equally connected to domestic animals. Deer and cattle are her special animals in mythology and could be used to represent her. Her nature in mythology seems to be both motherly, with her many children and connection to milk and milking, and also sensual in her role as the lover of Fergus. She also is clearly a deity of abundance and sustenance, who provides for all who rely on her. Offerings to Flidais should include milk or any product created from milk, such as cheese, yoghurt, or butter.

1. O hOgain, 2006
2. Monaghan, 2004
3. Leahy, 1906
4. Macalister, 1941; Gwynne, 1906
5. *Leabor na h-Uidre*, nd
6. Macalister, 1941; Leahy, 1906
7. Keating, 1857
8. O hOgain, 2006
9. *Leabar na h-Uidre*, nd
10. *Banshenchus*, nd

Fotla

Also spelled Fódla, Fodhla, or Fohla, she is another eponymous sovereignty Goddess of Ireland. Her name may be related to an archaic term for grassy land[1]. Like her sisters she is associated with sovereignty and the land itself.

Her mother was either Eirnin or Ernmas, depending on the

source, and her sisters were Banba and Eriu[2]. Her father was Delbeath and her other sisters were the Morrigan, Macha, and Badb. Her husband was the warrior Mac Cécht, who was also one of the kings of the Tuatha Dé Danann and she was said to be the consort of Detar, which may or may not be another name for Mac Cécht[3].

Fotla met the invading Gaels at Slieve Felim in Limerick and asked that Ireland always bear her name; although less common today Fotla is still a poetic name for the island[4]. Daragh Smyth relates her to the sovereignty of warriors of Ireland.

Those who wish to connect to Ireland itself, the land or the people, may choose to honor or connect to Fotla. You may decide to do this in any way that involves learning about or respecting Irish history, language, or culture. Offerings to her might include any of the traditional ones, such as milk, butter, or grain.

1. MacKillop, 1998
2. O hOgain, 2006
3. Smyth, 1988; *Banshenchus*, n.d.
4. MacKillop, 1998

Macha

Macha's name may mean plain or field, relating her to the land and sovereignty[1]. The word in Old Irish has a variety of meanings including royston crow, milking yard/field, and field or plain. In modern Irish the word means cattle field or yard, a fine group of cattle in a pasture, or, when added to brea bo, a herd[2]. In the Dindshenchus it is said that Macha's other name is Grian: 'her two names, not seldom heard in the west, were bright Grian and pure Macha' and 'in the west she was Grian, the sun of womankind.'[3]. The word Grian itself has multiple meanings including: sun, shining, bright, radiant, and luminary.

Macha is one of the Tuatha Dé Danann who appears in several different places in Irish mythology in different guises, not all of them obviously divine. However, scholars tend to agree that these different appearances share a common thread and that there is a pattern between them that shows her to be a single divine being in different stories. She appears among the people of Partholon, once as one of the Nemedians, as one of the Tuatha Dé Danann, as a 'fairy woman' and as a queen. There is no agreement about exactly which of these five appearances are related to each other and how, with different scholars having differing opinions, so all will be presented here.

Because of her multiple mythic appearances her parentage is convoluted. She is a daughter of Partholon in one story, and of Sainrith mac Imbaith in another[4]. As one of the Tuatha Dé Danann she is a daughter of Ernmas and Delbeath, sister to Badb and the Morrigan. Some people consider these three sisters to make up the triple Morrigan; in the *Lebor Gabala Erenn* it says 'Delbaeth...has three daughters, the famous war-furies Badb, Macha, and Mórrígu.'[5]. In some sources, such as the *Sanas Cormac*, Macha herself is called Morrigan, as it is both a name and title. Among the Gods she may also be the wife of Nuada Agatlamh[6]. In her other myths her husbands are Nemed, Crunnchu, and Cimbaeth. Her children are Fial and Fer[7].

In the first story she is listed among the people of Partholon, the second settlement of Ireland, but we are told nothing else about her. The people of Partholon die of a plague.

Next she appears as the wife of Nemed, of the third race to settle Ireland, and in this tale she dies clearing the plains of Ireland for farming[8]. In alternate versions she clears the land and then has a prophetic vision of the death and destruction of the future *Tain Bo Cuiligne*, which causes her to die of a broken heart or in yet another version her husband cleared the land and she died there so he named it for her[9]. These stories have cosmogenical significance and link her to the creation of the Earth as well as to its produce. This fits a pattern of Irish Goddesses who clear land in exchange for making room for civilization and settlement and sacrifice their lives in the process. The connection of the meaning of her name to cows and milking as well as fields and pasture relates to her as a land Goddess and fits the symbolism of the Nemedian story.

As one of the Tuatha Dé Danann, Macha appears accompanying the men to battle in the first *Cath Maige Tuired* and in the second, the battle against the Fomorians, it is said that she fell in battle with Nuada at the hands of Balor of the evil eye[10]. In the first battle of Maige Tuired she also acts with her two sisters, Badb and the Morrigan, to use magic against the specifically by sending rain, fog, and showers of blood and fire upon the opposing army; the second battle of Mag Tuired lists the three Morrigan as ban-draoithe, or Druids[11]. This tells us that not only is she a warrior, but also a magic user, especially of battle magic.

Next she appears as a fairy woman who marries a peasant named Crunnchu, and becomes pregnant with twins. He goes to a festival held by the king who is bragging of the speed of his horses. Crunnchu, despite being warned by Macha not to speak of her to anyone else, brags that his wife could outrace any horse, and the furious king demands that Crunnchu bring her immediately to race or forfeit his life. Macha begs for a delay as she is in labor, but is denied and forced to race anyway. She wins, collapsing and birthing her twins just past the finish line and curses the men of Ulster with nine days of labor pain in their greatest hour of need for 'nine times nine' generations before dying (although in some versions of the story she doesn't die, but simply returns to the Otherworld because Crunnchu broke her prohibition). According to the *Metrical Dindshenchas*, Macha gives birth to a boy and girl named Fir and Fial[12]. To this day the spot carries her name, Emain Macha, where for a long time festivals and assemblies were held, especially at Lunasa[13].

In the final story she is Macha Mog Ruadh, Macha Red-Hair, daughter of one of three kings who share the rulership of Ireland, each ruling for seven years in turn. This Macha is listed as the 76th ruler of Ireland and said to have ruled around the 4th century BCE[14]. When her father dies, Macha steps up to rule, but is challenged by the other two kings who do not want to co-rule with a woman. She battles them and wins, and when her seven years are up she refuses to turn leadership over to the others since she is queen not by blood but through victory in battle. One of the two kings dies, leaving five sons who would challenge her, so she goes to them in the appearance of a crone or leper and seduces them one by one, tying them up afterwards and thereby defeating them and enslaving them. In some versions of the story she forces the five brothers to build her fort at Emhain Macha. Finally she marries the last of the original three kings, Cimbaeth. There is much mythic symbolism in this story including the number of kings and years, as well as Macha going to the five sons disguised as either a crone or leper, and then her marrying the final king to give him full sovereignty.

The severed heads of warriors, taken as trophies in battle, were called 'Mesrad Macha' or Macha's nut crop, further showing her role as a battle Goddess[15]. Macha is strongly associated with several animals including horses and crows. In the *Sanas Cormac* it is said that Macha is another word for crow. She possessed an Otherworldly horse named Liath Macha (Grey of Macha) which appeared out of the Otherworld to Cu Chulainn and was one of his chariot horses; before his death the Liath Macha wept prophetic tears of blood. She is also associated with horses because of her race against them as Macha the fairy woman, wife of Crunnchu. Her connection to horses may be a reflection of her role as a sovereignty Goddess, with the horse as a symbol of the rulership of the king[16]. Generally Macha is associated with horses, crows, battle, magic, sovereignty, justice, and the land. Macha is particularly associated with Ulster, and particularly Armagh (Ard Macha) and Navan Fort (Emain Macha). In the notes of the *Lebor Gabala Erenn* Macalister suggests that Macha was a later addition to the Badb/Morrigan pairing, saying,

'Macha, one of the Badb sisterhood, has a certain individuality of her own, and enjoyed a special cult, probably centered at Armagh (Ard Macha), to which she bequeathed her name.'[17].

Modern Irish pagans often associate Macha with issues relating to women, children, and justice, and some do relate her to pregnancy as well. I may add a bit of caution in approaching her during childbirth as in her mythology she did die that way. She is also often looked to as a Goddess of personal power and strength. Offerings to Macha can include oats, grains, bread, milk, whiskey, or weapons.

1. Sjoedstedt, 2000
2. O Donaill, 1977
3. Gwynn, 1924
4. Macalister, 1942; Gwynn, 1924
5. MacAlister, 1941
6. Ellis, 1987
7. Gwynn, 1924
8. Macalister, 1941
9. Green, 1992
10. Frazer, 1916; Gray, 1983
11. Gray, 1983
12. Gwynn, 1924
13. MacNeil, 1962
14. Ellis, 1987
15. Sjoedstedt, 2000
16. O hOgain, 2006
17. Macalister, 1941

The Morrigan

The name also appears as Morrigu, Morrigna, and Morrighan; in modern Irish it is Morríghan or Mór-ríoghain. Like several other Irish deity names it always appears with the definitive article prefix of 'the' before it. The meaning of the name Morrigan is somewhat disputed, but there are two main theories: firstly that it means, roughly, nightmare queen or queen of the dead – often given as phantom queen – and secondly that it means great queen[1]. The difference in meaning lies in where the accent mark, called a fada, is placed, but unfortunately Old Irish is notoriously irregular in its orthography so there is no clear cut answer to whether the first part of her name should be mor, meaning 'phantom' or mór meaning 'great, immense'. The name is applied not only to a specific singular Goddess, but also to other deities with similar purviews, being used as both a name and a title.

The Morrigan is the daughter of Ernmas and Delbeath and sister to Macha and Badb, as well as the sovereignty trio of Eriu, Fotla, and Banba. According to the *Lebor Gabala Erenn*: 'Ernmas had other daughters, Badb, and Macha, and Morrigu, whose name was Anand' while another redaction says: 'Delbaeth...has three daughters, the famous war-furies Badb, Macha, and Mórrígu, the latter sometimes called Anand or Danand.'[2]. This shows that the Morrigan's name could actually be Anand or Danand (Anu or Danu in the modern forms) and indeed both are given as her real name in various places. When the Anu connection is accepted some people further relate her to Áine, although that is mostly speculation[3]. She is the wife of the Dagda, and has one son, Meche, by an unnamed father; Meche had three serpents in his heart that could have destroyed all of Ireland so he was killed[4]. She is also said to have had a daughter, Adair, by the Dagda, and in some sources 26 daughters and 26 sons who were all warriors[5].

As a title several different Goddesses are referred to as the Morrigan in different places, and she often appears acting in conjunction with two other Goddesses with similar abilities, leading to the idea of a threefold Morrigan or triplicity of Morrigan Goddesses. Besides the Morrigan herself, both her sisters are called Morrigan as well and this trio of Morrigu, Badb, and Macha, are explicitly called 'the three Morrigans' in the *Sanas*

Cormac. The Goddesses Fea and Nemain are also sometimes called Morrigan, and can be interchanged with the previous named Morrigan to form the different Morrigan triplicities.

The Morrigan has many important appearances in mythology. In the first *Cath Maige Tuired* she and her sisters first attack the Fir Bolg with magic and then accompany the warriors to the battle-field several times, finally raising pillars on the field to prevent anyone from retreating so that the battle will be concluded. In mythology the Morrigan aids the Tuatha Dé Danann in fighting against both the Fir Bolg and the Fomorians by using magic to confound and weaken the enemy[6]. The *Banshenchus* calls her 'Morrigan, powerful in sorcery' and we see many examples of this including her punishing of the woman Odras by turning her into water[7]. This can also be seen in her using magic to weaken the Fomorian King Indech in the *Cath Maige Tuired*, as she promised the Dagda she would do before the battle, by taking two handfuls of his blood and 'the courage of his heart and kidneys of his valor'. In that same story when Lugh asks her what she will contribute to the fight she replies: "Not hard to say,' ... 'I have stood fast; I shall pursue what was watched; I will be able to kill; I will be able to destroy those who might be subdued."[8]. At the end of that fight it was said: 'Then the Morrigu, daughter of Ernmass, came, and heartened the Tuatha Dé to fight the battle fiercely and fervently. Thereafter the battle became a rout, and the Fomorians were beaten back to the sea.'[9]. She is skilled in magic, but she is also a fierce fighter herself and also skilled in the power of incitement. At the very end of that battle she also gives two great prophecies, one of good things to come and one of ill-tidings, showing that she is a skilled seer as well[10].

In *The Ulster Cycle*, she is the main force behind the actions that cause the cattle raid of Cúailgne, and acts to both hinder and help the hero Cú Chulainn. She steals a cow from a fairy hill and brings it to Ulster to be bred by a famous bull there, the Brown Bull of Cúailgne; it is the calf of this cow that will have a part in later inciting the two bulls to fight each other. As well, when she is returning with the cow to Connacht she meets Cú Chulain and the two engage in a battle of words where she foretells the cattle raid of Cúailgne and predicts that she will appear when he is fighting and hinder him. This later comes to pass in that story, when she attacks Cu Chulainn while he is fighting in a ford; she comes at him three times, once in the shape of an eel, once as a wolf, and once as a heifer. Each time she is injured by him and because he is half-Dé Danann himself she must trick him into healing her by giving her his blessing. She does this three times by appearing as a withered old woman with a cow and offering him fresh milk; every time he drinks he blesses her in thanks. In the cattle raid of Cúailgne the Morrigan also appears to incite the different armies, particularly at the final battle where she is seen in dream visions by the leaders of each force chanting incitements to them.

The Morrigan has many guises and appears in many forms. The most well-known is probably that of a crow or raven, a form she assumes in several myths including the stories of *The Ulster Cycle*. She can be a beautiful young woman or a half-blind old crone, a black bird, a wolf, an eel, or a cow, and often shifts between shapes in a single story. In the story of the Tain Bó Regamna she appears as a red haired woman, dressed in red, in a chariot pulled by a single-legged red horse. She appeared before the battle of Mag Rath as a naked, gray haired old woman who flew over the battlefield and lept from spear point to shield rim of the soldiers who would win the battle during the fight[11].

Many locations in Ireland are associated with the Morrigan or named for her. The river ford known as the 'Bed of the Couple' is named for her Samhain tryst with the Dagda from the *Cath Maige Tuired*. Gort na Morrigna, field of the Morrigan, in county Louth is hers as is Fulacht na Morrigna, Morrigan's Hearth, in County Tipperary[12]. In the Bóyne valley Mur na Morrigna, mound of the Morrigan, is also hers as well as Da Chich na Morrigna, the Paps of the Morrigan[13]. The cave of Cruachan, also called Uaimh na gCait or Oweynagat (cave of cats) is also especially associated with her, and is the site of another of her cattle stealing episodes, the one associated with Odras in the Dinshenchas.

The Morrigan is associated with war, battle, and death, certainly, but also with victory, strategy, magic, and possibly sovereignty, although not everyone agrees with her as a sovereignty Goddess. Several authors connect her to sovereignty through her connection to cattle and cattle raiding and O hOgain sees her as both a land and mother Goddess, although his view is not common. She incites warriors to fight and also terrifies those she has set herself against. Her strongest associations are clearly with warfare and also with fate so that some people have connected her to the Norse Valkyries[14].

Modern pagans choose to honor the Morrigan for a wide variety of reasons including her relation to prophecy, magic, and success. Some pagans in the military choose to connect to her due to her mythic association with war, battle, and warriors. Witches sometimes relate to her for her magical skill. Offerings to the Morrigan can include milk, cream, butter, weapons, whiskey, and some people do choose to offer her blood, although that can be controversial.

1. eDIL, n.d.
2. MacAlister, 1941
3. Ellis, 1987; Jones, 2009
4. Gwynn, 1924
5. Gray, 1983
6. Gray, 1983; O hOgain, 2006
7. Gwynn, 1924; *Banshenchus*, n.d.
8. Gray, 1983
9. Cross & Slover, 1936
10. Gray, 1983
11. Smyth, 1988

12. ibid
13. Smyth, 1988; O hOgain, 2006
14. Jones, 2009

Nemain

Nemain, also called Neman, Nemon, or Nemhain; her name possibly means venomous or frenzy[1]. However, the etymology is highly speculative and uncertain. *O'Clery's Glossary* gives us, 'Nemain, that is madness or insanity' (this could also be translated as 'Nemain that is fury or terror.') and an entry in *Cormac's Glossary* gives us: 'Be Neit, that is Neit the name of the man. The woman Nemain his wife. They are a poisonous couple indeed'. Although these glossaries are more fanciful in their meanings than factual they do show that the association between her name and the idea of her being venomous and inciting madness or frenzy is very old.

Nemain is said to be the daughter of Elcmar, the original owner of Brugh na Bóyne and possibly an alternate name of Nuada. She is the sister of Fea and wife of Neit, an obscure God of war, although the phrase Bé Neit, which is translated wife of Neit, can also mean woman of war or battle and appears elsewhere as a name in its own right. To add to the confusion on this issue some sources describe her as the wife of Nuada and conflate her with Macha, while others describe her as an aspect of Badb[2]. In the *Lebor Gabala Erenn* we are told that Badb and Nemain are two wives of Net: 'Net son of Indui, his two wives, Badb and Nemain without falsehood'[3]. In another version we are told that it is Fea and Nemain who are his wives and that they are sisters, daughters of Elcmar: 'Fea and Nemain: two wives of Net son of Indui, that is two daughters of Elcmar of the Brugh'[4]. Due to this Heijda suggests that Fea may be the name of Badb in the same way that Anand is for Morrigu[5]. Macalister agrees, suggesting that Fea and Nemain represent an earlier twin-pairing that evolved into the grouping of Badb and Nemain; he also suggests that Badb became a dyad with the Morrigu before becoming a triplicity with Morrigu and Macha.

In many modern popular books she can be found listed along with Badb and Macha as the three Morrigan, as if she were the Morrigu. Hennessey in his 1870 book *The Ancient Irish Goddess of War* seems to have been the first to say that the Morrigan triplicity consisted of Badb, Macha, and Nemain, something that has often been repeated since. Heijda favors the idea of Nemain as an alternate name for Badb or as a Goddess paired with Badb separate from the Morrigan. The equating of Nemain and Badb is common and can be found in multiple sources where the two names are treated as interchangeable, although the two also appear together fairly often.

The primary source we have for Nemain in mythology is the *Tain Bo Cuiligne*. At one point in the story Cu Chulainn shouts and arouses the supernatural forces, after which Nemain appears and 'intoxicates the army there'[6]. In another recension of the story we see Nemain appearing with Badb and Be Neit, shrieking and terrifying the gathered army. Heijda suggests that it is quite likely that due to a scribal error instead of 'Badb *and* Be Neit and Nemain' this passage should read 'Badb *that is* Be Neit and Nemain'[7]. This is entirely logical as Be Neit rarely appears anywhere as an individual being and in the glossaries is usually equated with either Badb or the Morrigan, and sometimes Nemain. In point of fact the name Be Neit simply means woman of battle or wife of Net and may be a general term used to describe war Goddesses rather than a proper name, which would also explain why in glossary entries she is so often immediately equated to another named deity. Towards the end of the story we see Nemain appearing alone in a similar occurrence to the first, bringing what is described as 'intoxication' on the army there so that warriors fell on their own swords and spears and a hundred died[8].

In *O'Mulconry's Glossary* we are told: 'Red Nemain, that is heat of a fire, that is: red Nemain passion and the rest'. It is interesting that O'Mulconry associates Nemain with both fire and passion, adding a layer of depth to her usual associations. It is also quite interesting that he calls her 'Nemain derga' – red Nemain – as this is a common name given to Badb, who is called the red Badb and the red-mouthed Badb. Additionally we know that Nemain was a magic worker for the Tuatha Dé Danann[9]. Nemain is also called 'wise in poetry' in the *Lebor Gabala Erenn*. In one source she is called beautiful and described as a judge[10]. Almost all descriptions of her mention battle and war.

Overall it seems clear she was associated Badb and Fea, and was called both Badb and Be Neit herself. She does often appear acting with Badb though, suggesting that when she is called Badb it is being used as a title, rather than that she herself is Badb. We know she was one of the sorceresses of the Tuatha Dé Danann and also that she was said to be wise in poetry and 'without falsehood', and *Cormac's Glossary* calls her poisonous. When we see her appearing in stories in an active role, she is a bringer of 'mesc', that is drunkenness, intoxication, and confusion, which is directly associated with her terrifying cry that causes terror in those who hear it, and brings such panic that people fall on their own weapons or kill their comrades. She is madness, insanity, frenzy, and perhaps the passion of battle. Whether or not she was one of the Morrigan, per se, she was without doubt a Goddess of war and battle, and strongly associated with Badb. It does seem likely when looking at the total of the gathered material that Nemain originally formed a war Goddess pair with Badb, as the two are often associated with each other and act together, and Nemain is given the title of Badb as well as Morrigan.

People might choose to honor Nemain as a bringer of victory or as a Goddess of sorcery. She may also be invoked in conjunction with Badb or with the God Neit. Traditional offerings for the Tuatha Dé Danann would be good for Nemain, including butter, milk and grain or bread.

1. Ellis, 1987; Green, 1992
2. Ellis, 1987; O hOgain, 2006
3. Macalister, 1941
4. ibid
5. Heijda, 2007
6. Windisch, 1905
7. Heijda, 2007
8. Windisch, 1905
9. *Banshenchus*, n.d.
10. Gulermovich Epstein, 1998

Chapter 3

Other Gods of Ireland

Among Irish pagans by far the most popular deities honored are those found among the ranks of the Tuatha Dé Danann. However, other figures from myths are sometimes worshipped in modern practice as well, drawn from the ranks of the Fomorians as well as those few who have no clear group allegiance. These deities are often more primal in nature and may represent powers of entropy or chaos, particularly the Fomorians. The people who honor them today seem to be drawn to them with the idea that they are older pre-Celtic deities with beneficial aspects. In this chapter we will look at a selection of the more popular non-Tuatha Dé Danann deities.

Crom Cruach

One of the more interesting non-Tuatha Dé Danann deities that some people choose to honor today is Crom Cruach, synonymous according to scholars with Cenn Cruiach, and likely also the same as Crom Dubh[1]. Crom means bent, stooped or crooked; cruach has a wider array of meanings including stack of corn; rick; heap, conical pile, gory, bloody; high-colored; bloodthirsty, slaughter, wounding, carnage[2]. The meaning of Crom Cruach's name is uncertain, but many people seem to read it as either 'bent bloody one' or 'crooked heap'. Cenn Cruiach may mean 'head of the hill'[3]. Crom Dubh may mean 'black stooped one' or 'dark croucher' and Daithi O hOgain believes all the different iterations of Crom are actually derived from Christian imagery and that the deity himself is a later literary invention. In contrast, Daragh Smyth sticks with the mythic and pseudo-historic suggestion that Crom was the primary God of the pagan Irish before the conversion.

Crom's parentage and family relationships are unknown. For the three days of Lunasa the Goddess Áine is Crom's consort, and she herself takes on a more fierce aspect to match him[4].

In modern folklore many Lunasa celebrations center on the defeat of Crom by Saint Patrick, often on the last Sunday in July or first in Sunday August, which is called Domhnach Chroim Duibh – 'Crom Dubh Sunday'[5]. Marian MacNeill believes that these stories likely reflect older pagan stories that would have pitted Lugh against Crom, where Lugh must secure the harvest for the people, but that after Christianization the Catholic saint replaced the Tuatha Dé Danann God. Crom at Lunasa represents the primal force that is either trying to steal the harvest or keep the harvest and with whom a hero must contend to secure supplies for the community. Many of the myths relating to Lugh and Crom Dubh, who is sometimes called Crom Cruach, involve Lugh battling and outwitting Crom and thus insuring the safety and bounty of the harvest; in some cases this theme is given the additional layer of the defeat, sacrifice, consumption, and then resurrection of Crom's bull, which may argue for an older element of bull sacrifice on this day[6].

Besides Lunasa, Crom is strongly associated with Samhain when it was said he was honored at Mag Slecht in County Cavan with offerings of the firstborn of every living thing in exchange for a good harvest of corn and milk. According to the *Rennes Dindshenchas*, three-quarters of the people who bowed down to him died[7]. In the *Metrical Dindshenchas* we are told that Crom was the primary God of the pagan Irish, who was honored on Samhain, and that they offered him one third of their children in exchange for a good harvest of milk and grain[8]. This entry also tells the story of Saint Patrick's destruction of Crom's golden statue at Mag Slecht along with the 12 stone statues surrounding it. According to another story in a late version of Saint Patrick's life the saint overthrew Crom, possibly under the name of Cenn Cruaich, whose statue of gold-embossed stone was at Mag Slecht surrounded by 12 silver-embossed statues[9]. In some versions he ordered Crom's statue to be buried after destroying it. Of course, given the shifting that MacNeill speculates occurred at Lunasa between Lugh and Saint Patrick battling Crom, one does wonder if perhaps it wasn't Lugh who originally confronted and destroyed Crom's statue at Mag Slecht, or if these stories reflect an older tale of a battle between the two similar to the tales from Lunasa. Several scholars, including MacNeill and Smyth, suggest a possible connection between Crom and Lugh's Fomorian grandfather Balor. According to this theory, Crom is in fact Balor by another name, and the story of Saint Patrick and Crom Cruach battling over the harvest is a thinly disguised version of an older tale of Balor and Lugh's combat.

The worship of Crom at Mag Slecht is mentioned in two other sources as well, the *Annals of the Four Masters* and Keating's *Foras Feasa ar Éirinn*, both of which also name Samhain as the main date of his worship and state that Crom was the main deity of Ireland. Unlike the two Dindshenchas versions, neither of these suggest a direct connection between Crom's worship and the deaths of three-quarters of the men honoring him at Samhain. Keating also specifies that it was the pseudo-historical king Tigernmas who introduced Crom's worship to Ireland, placing that occurrence about 1200 BCE[10].

In the later stories Crom is recast as a human pagan who goes to Saint Patrick to be saved or is otherwise converted by him[11]. This follows the pattern seen in Irish myth more generally where the oldest version of a character is either implicitly or explicitly divine, then is recast as Otherworldly, and finally as human. The same progression can be seen, for example, with Áine who is originally described as one of the Tuatha Dé Danann, then as a woman of the sí, and finally as a mortal girl.

I am aware of some modern Irish pagans who see Crom as a pre-Celtic agricultural God. Crom Cruach is often portrayed by modern Irish pagans who honor him as a God of the harvest or of the grain. They choose to honor him as a bringer or protector of the harvest rather than see him as a cthonic or chaotic force that must be fought against. In this view he is placed alongside the older Gods like the Cailleach as reflecting what could possibly be an echo of Neolithic paganism, but of course this is impossible to prove. The only thing that is clear in mythology is that he was offered to during the harvest so that he would not harm or keep it, had an association with death, and was viewed as an enemy of Lugh and consort of Áine. He is a complex deity who maintained his adversarial role after the conversion even when the name of his adversary changed. Whatever else Crom is or may be we can perhaps say that he represents an eternal struggle to successfully gain the harvest and pay the cost for what we need to survive the winter.

Offerings to him might include grain, alcohol, milk, or a shared meal.

1. Smyth, 1988; O hOgain, 2006; MacNeill, 1962
2. eDIL, n.d.
3. MacNeill, 1962
4. MacNeill, 1962
5. Smyth, 1988
6. MacNeill, 1962
7. Stokes, 1895
8. Gwyn, 1924
9. Smyth, 1988; O hOgain, 2006
10. Keating, 1854
11. MacNeill, 1962

The Cailleach

The Cailleach, or Caillech in Old Irish, is a complex deity who seems to have roots in Neolithic Ireland. Cailleach is from a word that means 'veiled woman' or 'elderly woman', but in later usage was a pejorative generally used to mean hag or witch. She is called the Cailleach Beara or Beare for the Beara peninsula, which is her main habitation, although in folklore she is also sometimes given the epithet of Béarrach; the Old Irish word berach means sharp or horned. The Cailleach Beara's true name is said to be Buí, a word that may mean 'yellow'[1]. Alternately it may originally have been Boí, a word related to the one for cow (bó) and it's possible that she was at one time a cow Goddess who represented the land and its sovereignty on the Beara peninsula[2]. This idea is somewhat supported by her legendary possession of a powerful bull, the Tarbh Conraidh, who had only to bellow to get a cow with calf. Certainly she is strongly associated with Beara and because of the irregular orthography of Old Irish either version of her name is possible, although Buí is better attested, appearing in the well-known poem The Lament of the Old Woman of Beare. MacKillop suggests that she may also previously have been known as Dígde, a sovereignty Goddess of Munster, and Duineach whose name he gives as meaning '[having] many followers', both of which were subsumed into the single identity of the Cailleach Beara at some point[3].

Several different Goddesses are called 'Cailleach' in Irish myth including the Cailleach Beara of Cork and Cailleach Gearagáin of county Cavan[4]. The most well known, however, is the Cailleach Beara, who is strongly associated with south west Ireland. She is considered a sovereignty figure, the archetypal crone who appears offering the throne to a potential king in exchange for intimacy; those who reject her in this guise will never rule, but those who embrace her as an old woman will find her transformed into a beautiful young woman and will themselves become king. She is also credited with creating many of the standing stones and geographic features in various areas, who folklore claims are people or animals that she transformed; her bull the Tarbh Conraidh, for example, was turned into a stone in a river by her when he tried to swim across it to reach a herd of cows on the other side. In other parts of Ireland, including

Connacht, Leinster, and Ulster, the Cailleach Beara is seen as the spirit of the harvest who inhabits the grain and flees from the scythes in the form of a hare[5]. In many areas harvest traditions included the practice of leaving the final sheaf standing in the field and naming it the Cailleach.

The Cailleach as Buí is said to be one of the four wives of Lugh, although other sources say that she had seven husbands; she is also said to have had 50 foster children[6]. The Cailleach is generally described as an old woman, but she also can appear young, and is considered the progenitor of some family lines including the Corca Duibhne[7]. A 10th century poem says that she was the lover of the warrior Fothadh Canainne. Folklore claims that she has two sisters, also named Cailleach of their respective areas, who live in Dingle and Iveragh[8].

It is said that the Sliab na gCailligh in county Meath were created when the Cailleach flew over the area and accidently dropped the stones[9]. She is strongly associated with several areas in Ireland including the Beara peninsula in Munster and Slieve Daeane in Connacht[10].

The Cailleach may be honored for a variety of personal reasons, and some choose to honor her as a Goddess of sovereignty and power. She is also sometimes honored as a Goddess of winter and storms, although this borrows somewhat from the Scottish view of her. I have success calling on her for protection of myself and my home during winter storms. Certainly she can be connected to as a deity of the harvest, prosperity, and the power of age. Offerings to her can include whiskey, grain, or milk.

1. Murphy, 1956
2. O hOgain, 2006
3. MacKillop, 1998
4. Smyth, 1988
5. O hOgain, 2006

6. MacKillop, 1998
7. Smyth, 1988
8. O hOgain, 2006
9. Smyth, 1988
10. MacKillop, 1998

Donn

According to Green, Donn's name means 'Dark One'; however, looking up the Old Irish we see a variety of meanings for the word donn including brown, noble, poet, stolen property, pregnant, and ale[1]. The dictionary also defines Donn as: 'Probably the God of the dead or the ancestral father to whom all are called at their death; Amalgamated with the Christian Devil'[2].

In the *Lebor Gabala Erenn* Donn is one of the sons of Mil who invades Ireland with his brothers, displacing the Tuatha Dé Danann after a great battle. Donn, however, is killed beforehand. There are a variety of explanations for why Donn died. Some Irish pagans say that it is because he insulted the sovereignty Goddess Eriu when the Milesians were negotiating with her by claiming his people did not need any Gods but the ones they already had. Others say Eriu only predicted his doom, but did not cause it[3]. In one version of the story, Donn becomes frustrated with the slow progress of the invasion and threatens to put to the sword every living thing in Ireland at which time the wind rises up and drowns him, but in another version of the story the Tuatha Dé Danann had sent a plague upon the ships of the Milesians and Donn offers himself as a willing sacrifice to save all the others[4]. In both cases his body is interred on a great rocky prominence which is then named Tech Duinn (Donn's house).

Both Green and Jones compare Donn to the Roman Dis Pater, who Caesar said the Gauls believed they descended from; as Donn was seen to be an ancestor of the Gaels and also a deity of the land of the dead, this comparison seems valid. Green goes further in saying that Donn is likely also Da Derga, who appears according to her as a death God in the story of Da Derga's Hostel[5]. Ellis suggests that Donn might also relate to Dagda and Bile, while O hOgain agrees with the Dagda association, seeing the name Donn as originally an epithet most likely of the Dagda; he relates the name to the concept of darkness and the realm of the dead.

To this day Tech Duinn still bears Donn's name. It is located off the southwest coast of Cork in Ireland, and also goes by the name of Bull Rock. Tech Duinn in folklore is seen as the entrance to the Otherworldly land of the dead, where all the dead must pass, and Donn himself is the God of the underworld and first ancestor in part because he was the first human acknowledged to die in Ireland[6]. Donn is referred to as the King of the Dead in the *Death Tale of Conaire* and in a 9th century text Donn claims that all the dead go to his house[7]. Folklore tells us that Tech Duinn is a place where the dead go, but not necessarily their final destination; some believe that the house of Donn is where the dead go before moving on to the Otherworld[8]. In the 8th to 10th centuries, Tech Duinn was seen as an assembly place of the dead, and a place that the dead both went to and left from[9]. Besides Tech Duinn in County Cork, Donn is also connected to Cnoc Firinne in county Limerick and Dumhcha in County Clare.

The Donn of Cnoc Firinne had strong aspects of a lord of the aos sidhe, being called Donn Firinne and said to kidnap people into his hill who had been thought to have died[10]. Like many other Irish deities belief in Donn seems to have survived conversion to Christianity by shifting him from God to Good Neighbor, albeit a very powerful one. In County Clare, Donn was Donn na Duimhche, Donn of the Dune, and was believed to ride out as a fairy horseman with his army[11].

Donn may or may not always have been seen as a deity but he certainly seems to have been understood as one from at least the 8th century onward, until his shift into an Otherworldly horseman. Throughout his shifting mythology, though, he has always been related to death and the dead, both as the Lord of the 'house' where the dead go and also as a primordial ancestor of the people. He also has a strong association to the sea, the drowned, and to horses. Modern Irish pagans tend to look to Donn most strongly as a God of the dead and the ancestors. He can be honored for anything relating to the dead or dying, connecting to ancestors, or honor Donn himself as keeper of the house of the dead. Offerings to him might include ale, water, silver, or food, and I have found him receptive to coffee.

1. Green, 1997; eDIL, n.d
2. eDIL, n.d
3. Berresford Ellis, 1987
4. Daimler, 2015
5. Green, 1997
6. Jones, 2004
7. O hOgain, 2006
8. Ellis, 1987
9. O hOgain, 2006
10. ibid
11. ibid

Manannán mac Lir

One of the deities that can be found in the mythology of several different Celtic nations is Manannán; called Manannán mac Lir (Manannán son of the sea). His home was said to be the Isle of Man, called Manu in Irish; Manannán's name clearly derives from this and since this name for the island is a later development O hOgain posits that Manannán himself and his mythology are later developments as well, likely dating to no earlier than the 3rd century CE[1]. The Irish initially borrowed the name from the Welsh, but then added the title 'mac Lir', which was then borrowed into the Welsh as 'map Llyr'[2]. This demonstrates the composite nature of Manannán that has developed over time as the related Celtic cultures shared mythology back and forth. To the Manx he was the first king of the Island of Man, and stories locate his grave there, as well as tell of how he would walk among the Manx fishermen as they repaired their nets[3]. A Manx poem describes how the inhabitants of the island would pay rent to the God every year, as he was the owner of the island, and they were his tenants[4].

Manannán's appearance is described as being that of a handsome warrior[5]. Manannán's wife is Fand, a peerless beauty who at one point had an affair with Cu Chulain, until Manannán used his magic to make Cu Chulainn forget about her and return to his own wife, Emer. It is said that Manannán traveled to the mortal world to father Mongán, a prince and hero, and under the name of Oirbsiu he may have fathered the Conmhaicne sept of Leinster[6]. There are many stories about his various sons and daughters, who are usually treated as minor characters; he also has a variety of foster children including Eógabal, Fer I, and Lugh[7]. One of his more well-known children is Áine, although some sources list her as his wife instead of child.

Manannán was originally said to live on the Isle of Man, a place which was seen as near mythical in Irish stories; later his home shifted fully into the Otherworld, to Eamhain[8]. The Irish described Eamhain in rich detail as a sacred place, an island held up by four silver legs or pillars, on which grew magical apples which gave the island the full name of Eamhain Abhlach, Eamhain of the Apples[9]. Other names for his domain include Mag Meall (the pleasant plain) and Tír Tairngire (the land of promise). Each of these names and associations reflect the connection between Manannán's realm and the Otherworld.

Manannán was a God of the ocean for whom the waves were as solid as land, and he was known to control the weather and had a reputation as a skilled magician. He possessed a special horse named Enbharr (water foam) who ran over the ocean as if it were land, and all the waves were said to be his horses, just as the fish were called his livestock, compared to sheep and cows; he also had a variety of magical birds and hounds, as well as magical pigs that could be eaten one day and revived to life the next[10]. He also owned a magical sword, Frecraid (answerer), which no armor could stand against[11]. In the story of his meeting with king Cormac mac Art he is described as carrying a golden apple branch that rang with sweet music that could soothe people to sleep or heal the ill and wounded[12]. Some sources consider him a shapeshifter, and his magical powers were numerous; he could travel faster than the wind could blow in his magical boat, he could create realistic illusions, and he had a cloak of forgetfulness that would take the memory from a person[13]. It was this cloak that he used to cause Cu Chulainn to forget Fand in the story of the Only Jealousy of Emer. He possesses a magical crane bag that contains a variety of powerful items[14].

Manannán is sometimes counted among the Tuatha Dé Danann and sometimes viewed as an outsider deity. He was not including among the people of Danu in mythology until the 10th century and his role in stories is often that of an adviser or magician. According to one version, when the Gods are defeated by the Gaels and retreat into the sí it is Manannán who assigns each new home to the Gods[15]. He gives three gifts to the Gods: the féth fiadha, the feast of Goibhniu, and the pigs of Manannán[16]. The féth fiadha was either a spell or cloak that allowed the person to become invisible and travel unnoticed. The feast of Goibhniu was a magical feast that kept the Gods young and living. And the pigs of Manannán were immortal swine who could be killed and would return to life.

Manannán's nature is as mercurial as the sea. When visiting Elcmar at his sí he is paid great tribute with rushes laid out before him and a great feast prepared, yet despite the pleasant visit he dislikes Elcmar and acts against him later[17]. In the stories of the

Fianna Manannán is often helpful, yet also appears at least once to stir strife and create trouble among the warriors[18]. This could reflect the knowledge of all sailors that the favor of the sea is fickle and quick to change, or perhaps Manannán's own liminal nature tends toward changeability.

His special holiday is midsummer, the date on which the people of the Isle of Man would make offerings to him to pay their rent[19]. In several sources rushes are mentioned as offerings for him, so it could be safely assumed that rushes were historically sacred to him[20]. The sea and waters were also strongly associated with him, and it said in the story of Oirbsiu that when he died a lake burst forth from his grave. He is also strongly associated with horses and apples. Many modern neo-Druids see Manannán as the keeper of the gates between our world and the Otherworld and call on him to open the way between the worlds.

People seeking to honor Manannán today may want to spend time by or near the ocean. He can be sought out and honored as a deity of magical power, wisdom, guidance, and strategy. Offerings to Manannán could include ale, beer, pork, apples, rushes, broom (the herb), or silver.

1. O hOgain, 2006
2. ibid
3. Monaghan, 2004
4. MacQuarrie, 1997
5. Ellis, 1987
6. O hOgain, 2006
7. O hOgain, 2006; MacKillop, 1998
8. O hOgain, 2006
9. ibid
10. O hOgain, 2006; MacKillop, 1998
11. MacKillop, 1998
12. O hOgain, 2006
13. Monaghan, 2004; MacKillop, 1998

14. MacKillop, 1998
15. O hOgain, 2006
16. ibid
17. O hOgain, 2006
18. ibid
19. Macquarrie, 1997
20. Macquarrie, 1997; O hOgain, 2006

Medb

Medb, also spelled Meadhbh, Méadhbh, Meave. Meav, Meave, or Maive. Often translated as 'She who intoxicates', her name literally means 'strong, intoxicating' and is closely related to the adjective 'medach' (relating to or abundant in mead) and the word for mead itself 'mid'[1]. In early Irish myth kingship was conveyed by the appearance of an Otherworldly woman who would offer the potential king a cup of mead or ale to drink[2]. Medb is sometimes given the epithet of 'Lethderg' (half-red) although by some accounts Medb Lethderg may be a separate character; it is possible, however, that the Medb of this name who is based in Teamhair, where Medb of Connacht was raised, is the same personage.

Medb's mother is often named as Cruacha, from whom Medb's fort at Cruachan is named, and her father is Eochaid Feidlech; she had two sisters, Eithne and Clothru, the second of whom Medb killed[3]. She is the wife of several kings including Conchobar Mac Nessa, King of Ulster, and Ailill king of Connacht, as well as two other Connacht kings, Tinde mac Conra Cas and Eochaid Dála. She was also well known for her penchant for taking lovers, including famous warrior Fergus mac Róich, and it was claimed that it took 32 men to satisfy her[4]. She had seven sons with Ailill, all of whom she renamed Maine to fulfill a prophecy that said a son of hers by that name would kill Conchobar. She had three daughters named Finnabair, Cainder and Faife, of which Finnabair was the best known for her role in the story of the cattle raid of Cúailgne[5]. She also had two children by Fergus, named Ciarrai and Conmac.

Her greatest mythic appearance is in *The Ulster Cycle* where she starts the cattle raid of Cuiligne in order to obtain the Brown Bull of Ulster to prove that she and not her husband Ailill have the most possessions. This is essential for her because in Irish law the marriage partner with the greater wealth was the dominant partner and Medb by nature needed to be dominant. Although Ailill led the army with her, Medb was its true leader and made many of the key decisions with Ailill and Fergus advising her.

Medb is not counted among the numbers of the Tuatha Dé Danann, and is most often discussed as a human queen; however, her myths and description make her into the likely culmination of similarly named Goddesses of territory, sovereignty, and fertility[6]. Royal Irish Academy scholar T. F. O'Rahilly says of Medb: 'Leading characters in ancient Irish history such as…Medb are euphemerised divinities', firmly establishing that some do view her as Goddess[7]. She is a woman who always makes her own choices and who marries men who are or become kings, relating her to sovereignty. She is described as wearing a red cloak and with a bird or squirrel on her shoulder, holding a flaming spear in her hand, able to run faster than any horse and powerful enough that the sight of her can deprive men of two-thirds of their physical strength[8]. In later folklore she becomes a queen of the fairies just as many of the Tuatha Dé Danann Goddesses did.

Medb's strongest association is with Cruachan in county Roscommon, but she also has ties to Teamhair where it is said she was raised. Due to this Medb can be said to be associated with both Leinster and Connacht. Medb is also linked to a spot called Grianán Meidbe on an island in Lough Ree in Roscommon as well as Miscaun Maeve, or Maeve's cairn, in Sligo[9].

Medb is a powerful force, a pseudo-historical queen, a Goddess, a Fairy Queen. As a deity she is a Goddess of war, intoxication, sovereignty, territory (the people rather than the land itself perhaps), sexuality and fertility.

Modern Irish pagans may find many reasons to honor Medb, given her role as a powerful female and uncompromising ruler of her own power. Her symbols could be horses, birds, squirrels, spears, and cups or goblets. Offerings may include mead or any alcoholic beverage.

1. MacKillop, 1998; eDIL, n.d2O hOgain, 2006
2. MacKillop, 1998
3. Smyth, 1988
4. MacKillop, 1998
5. ibid
6. ibid
7. Smyth, 1988
8. MacKillop, 1998; Smyth, 1988
9. O Hogain, 2006

Neit

Neit or Nét, is a God whose name is from the word 'nia' meaning a warrior or champion. The *Sanas Cormaic* says that he is a God of war, and tells us that his wife is the Goddess Nemain, calling the couple 'poisonous'[1]. Neit is an obscure figure who is sometimes counted among the Fomorians and is often listed as the progenitor of both Fomorian and Tuatha Dé Danann figures. He was said to have a fortress at Aileach in Donegal[2].

In the *Lebor Gabala Erenn* we learn that he had two wives, either Fea and Nemain or Nemain and Badb, depending on which redaction you read[3].

1. *Sanas Cormaic*
2. O hOgain, 2006
3. Macalister, 1944

Tailtiu

Tailtiu, also Tailltiu and Tailte, was a queen of the Fir Bolg, a race of beings who held Ireland before the coming of the Tuatha Dé Danann. The Fir Bolg are the fourth group to settle Ireland, and like the Fomorians and Tuatha Dé Danann themselves, are said to be descendants of the third group of settlers, the Nemedians. By this genealogy the Fir Bolg and Tuatha Dé Danann have a shared ancestry, although in mythology they appear as enemies fighting over who will rule Ireland.

Tailtiu's father is sometimes said to be the King of Spain or she is said to be the child of either Mag Mór (great plain) or Umor Mor (large trough?) and her husband was the Fir Bolg King Eochaid mac Eirc[1]. Her foster son was Lugh, after he was given to her by his father Cian[2].

Tailtiu is a land Goddess with cosmogenic qualities, known for her effort to clear the plain of Meath in Ireland. The effort to do so was so great that she died in the process, asking her foster son Lugh, on her death bed, to institute commemorative games in her memory every year, which he did by creating the festival of Lunasa[3]. This effort to clear land to make it habitable and fit for civilization is a pattern that can be seen with some Irish Goddesses and may show echoes of an older creation myth that is now lost. In all the versions of such stories the Goddess clears an area so that it can be cultivated, making it suitable for her people and those coming after to live on, and the effort costs her her own life. Afterwards the area is named for the Goddess, forever reflecting her connection to it.

The commemorative games for her would become one of the four renowned fire festivals, Lunasa. In the original Old Irish the word, Lughnasadh, means 'funeral assembly of Lugh', named not for Lugh himself, but for his memorizing of Tailtiu. Later the word shifted to Lughnasa, and the meaning changed as well to 'games or assembly of Lugh'; the holiday was a time famous for assemblies and fairs, called aonacha in Irish, which included games of skill and horse racing[4]. Lunasa was one of the major holidays in ancient Ireland and was celebrated throughout the island; it was also a time for marriages called 'Teltown marriages', which could last only a year if the couple chose to separate after that time[5]. Traditionally Lunasa lasted for almost a full month, running for two weeks before August 1st and two weeks afterwards.

Tailtiu was associated with Meath and especially Telltown, between Navan and Kells. Telltown, of course, is the area Tailtiu cleared in myth and is said to be the best farmland in Ireland[6].

Modern pagans may choose to connect to Tailtiu as a primal earth Goddess or as a mother Goddess for her role as foster mother to Lugh. To some she takes on the role that Gaia plays in classical mythology, while to others she is a Goddess of the harvest and abundance because of her connection to Lunasa. Offerings to Tailtiu could include clear water, milk, and any food associated with the beginning of the harvest in August.

1. MacKillop, 1998; Smyth, 1988
2. Macalister, 1941
3. ibid
4. MacNeil, 1962
5. MacKillop, 1998
6. ibid

Chapter 4

Honoring the Irish Gods

One of the first questions people ask when they develop an interest in this spirituality is how to get started. This is a difficult question to answer, and indeed specific spiritual approaches will have their own guidelines. What follows here is just a rough outline and suggestions that may be applied, hopefully, to any spiritual path seeking to honor or connect to the Irish Gods. As such it is somewhat broad and general, but ideally will offer a place to start for people seeking a place to begin.

The absolute first step, truly, is to read. Read the mythology, the folklore, and the stories both old and modern to become familiar with the Gods and Spirits (aos sidhe aka Good Neighbors, or fairies) of Ireland. There is often a fine line at best between the Tuatha Dé Danann as Gods and the Aos Sidhe as fairies as could be seen by many of the entries in previous sections where a member of the Gods was later described as being a king or queen of fairy. Use this to get to know these Powers and to start to understand the worldview and cosmology. You can't read too much of this stuff, ever; however, never lose sight of the fact that many translations are older and suffer from the bias of the times they were written in. Try to read a variety of different versions of any one story to help you get the best perspective on it. It also helps to read not only the mythology and folklore, but also books about the culture of the pagan Irish to help provide a context for the stories. We can't read them and apply our modern standards and expectations to a world that existed hundreds or thousands of years ago and expect to fully understand the deeper meanings of the story. Use what you learn to build a framework of belief and practice in your own life.

Learn about the history of a specific deity that interest you.

Many of the Irish Gods have undergone interesting shifts and changes over time, as the new religion came in and the old was subsumed. Áine went from one of the Tuatha Dé Danann to a Fairy Queen to a mortal girl as her stories passed through time. Brighid went from a Goddess to a saint. Manannán was taken from an outside culture into the Tuatha Dé Danann, and then appeared in many stories as magician and trickster. Looking at any Irish deity usually shows a long and fascinating history, often including a journey through folk belief into modern times as a fairy or mortal. Although we often prefer to think of our Gods as strictly Gods it can provide a great deal of insight to study their places outside of divine roles as well.

Learn about the specific locations associated with the different Gods. One thing that is particularly true of the Irish Gods is that they are profoundly location based. The stories and folklore of the Gods include an array of sites and places that are intrinsically tied to the deities. It is far more difficult, perhaps even impossible on some level, to truly understand a deity without having some understanding of the locations that they lay claim to or that they give their name to.

If possible, travel to the locations you've learned about. Touch the places that the Gods themselves were said to have touched – still touch. See for yourself what the land looks like, what it feels like. Reading and studying about the places of the Gods is good, but actually going there and experiencing them yourself is better. It is impossible to fully imagine the scope and scale of sacred sites unless you are actually there.

Offer to the Gods to create reciprocity with these Powers. Offer in thanks and celebration, for blessing and protection. Offerings create a relationship between us and the Powers we honor that is important in our spirituality.

Connect to your spirituality regularly by celebrating holidays, reading, and essentially living your faith. Paganism of any kind isn't an occasional religion that you practice once in a while or a hobby, it's a way of life. If you want to connect to any deity it requires time and effort because it is a matter of building a relationship. To follow the Irish paganism in any sense one needs to first build a relationship with the Gods and then incorporate that into whatever religious or spiritual framework you use.

Try to set aside some space, no matter how small, in your home as a place for the Gods. Think about who and what the Gods are to you, and what part they play in your life. Why do you want to honor them? What is a God to you? Which Gods do you connect most strongly to and why? Who do you honor most often? While there are many Gods within the Irish pantheon there will be a selection of deities – perhaps as few as two or three, perhaps as many as a half dozen or more – that you are particularly drawn to for a variety of reasons. Over time these Gods will be the ones who you form the strongest connections to, much as each historic community had specific Gods within the wider pantheon that they honored.

Another important way to connect to the Gods is to connect to Irish culture; this can be done through language, music, food, studying social history, art, and literature. Being an Irish pagan is about more than just honoring the Irish Gods, it's also about a love of the culture those Gods come from. Although many people balk at the idea of learning the language even something as simple as learning a few words, or making the effort to learn how to properly pronounce the deities' names, can be helpful and make a person feel more connected. It's also much easier to understand the Gods when you understand the culture that they come from and are part of.

And there you have it. You can add seeking community in real life or online as well, but I think that the heart of honoring or connecting to the Irish Gods starts with you and your own life. If you aren't making the Irish Gods a part of your life in different ways then all the community participation in the world won't really help you. That isn't to downplay the importance of community, which is a wonderful source of support, but if you can't connect to the Gods without a community then you are missing the point altogether.

Since I mentioned reading, here is my basic recommended reading list. There are many, many other books that could be added to this list, but I tried to select books that represent an overview of the essential topics needed:

1. *The Sacred Isle* by Daithi O hOgain – discusses Irish religion from pre-Christian times through conversion.
2. *The Lebor Gabala Erenn* – the story of the invasions of Ireland by the Gods and spirits and eventually humans. This is the main text we have for the Tuatha Dé Danann's arrival in Ireland and contention against both the Fomorians and Gaels.
3. *Cath Maige Tuired* – the story of the battle of the Tuatha Dé Danann with the Fomorians. *The Cath Maige Tuired Cunga*, or First Battle of Maige Tuired is also worth reading.
4. *The Year in Ireland* by Kevin Danaher – an overview of holidays and folk practices throughout the year.
5. *Fairy and Folktales of the Irish Peasantry* by W. B. Yeats – a look at folklore and belief relating to the Fair Folk.
6. *Celtic Gods and Heroes* by M. Sjoestedt – discusses both the Gods, including the Irish ones, and tidbits of folklore and mythology. This book is useful both in understanding the Gods and practices and also in having a basis from which to build modern practices.
7. *Celtic Flame: An Insider's Guide to Irish Pagan Tradition* by Aedh Rua – one perspective on reconstructing the beliefs and practices of the pagan Irish in a modern setting. Although this approach will not be to everyone's taste it is a valuable example of how it can be done.
8. *A Child's Eye View of Irish Paganism* by Blackbird O'Connell – written for children aged eight to 12, this

book is an effective, short introduction to the basic beliefs, Gods, and practices of Irish paganism.

9. *A Practical Guide to Irish Spirituality* by Lora O'Brien – a really great, down-to-earth book about Irish spirituality from top to bottom by a modern Irish pagan. Probably the best single book you can read on the topic.

Conclusion

This book has made an effort to provide solid information on a variety of Irish deities, both common and less well known. Hopefully it will serve as a good resource for readers as well as a source of useful information. However, this book is only a small glimpse into a much larger world of Irish mythology; it should not in any way be considered an exhaustive work. Entire texts have been written on individual Irish deities, such as the Morrigan, Brighid, and Manannán, and it would be impossible to summarize that amount of information in a book the size of this one.

Irish mythology is a complex tapestry that tells the story not only of the Irish Gods, the Tuatha Dé Danann and other more primal beings, but also of the land of Ireland itself. The Gods are woven, literally, into the stones and mountains, the rivers and lakes, and they are just as present in the living landscape now as they were thousands of years ago. But they are also to be found in the written words of the old myths and the new folklore, in the lives and hearts of the people who worship them around the world. They are the Gods of Ireland and a part of Ireland itself, but they are also the Gods of the people who honor them, wherever those people may be found.

I wrote this because for many years I searched for this exact book: a text that would let me quickly look up basic information about Irish deities. I searched for it but I never found it, except in much larger versions that also included a lot of superfluous information I wasn't looking for or else were smaller but more generally Celtic and only touched on a half dozen or fewer of the most popular Irish Gods mixed in. My goal in putting this book out there was to provide a resource for others that I had always wanted for myself, and in the end I hope that has been achieved.

Bibliography

The Battle of Mag Mucrama http://www.maryjones.us/ctexts /mucrama.html

The Battle of Crimna http://www.maryjones.us/ctexts/cath crinna.html

Banshenchus (nd) Retrieved from http://www.maryjones.us/cte xts/banshenchus.html

Berresford, P., (1987) *A Dictionary of Irish Mythology*

Best, R., (2007) *The Settling of the Manor of Tara*

Calder, G., (1917) *Auraicept na N-Éces*

Carmicheal, A., (1900) *Carmina Gadelica*

Clark, R., (1991) *The Great Queens: Irish Goddesses from the Morrigan to Cathleen ní Houlihan*

Cross, T., and Slover. H., (1936) *Ancient Irish Tales*

Daimler, M., (2015) *Pagan Portals: Irish Paganism*

Daimler, M., (2015) *The Treasure of the Tuatha De Danann*

Daimler, M., (2015) *Tochmarc Etain* retrieved from http://lairbhan.blogspot.com/2015/09/tochmarc-etaine.html

Daimler, M., (2016) *Pagan Portals: Brigid*

eDIL (n.d.) *Electronic Dictionary of the Irish Language*

Ellis, P., (1987) *Dictionary of Irish Mythology*

Evans, D., (2011) http://www.celtnet.org.uk/gods_n/nudd.html

Frazer, J., (1916) *Cath Maige Tuired Cunga*

Gray, E., (1983) *Cath Maige Tuired*

Green, M., (1992) *Dictionary of Celtic Myth and Legend*

Gulermovich-Epstien, A., (1998) *War Goddess: The Morrigan and her Germano-Celtic Counterparts*

Gwynne E., (1906) *The Metrical Dindshenchas*

Gwynn, E., (1924) *Metrical Dindshenchas*

Heidja, K, (2007) *War-Goddesses, Furies, and Scald Crows: The Use of the Word Badb in Early Irish Literature*

Jones, M., (2009) Anu. Retrieved from http://www.maryjones

.us/jce/anu.html

Jones, M., (2012) Nodens. Retrieved from http://www.maryj ones.us/jce/nodens.html

Jones, M., (2004) Tech Duinn. Retrieved from http://www.maryj ones.us/jce/techduinn.html

Jones, M., (n.d.) *The Birth of Aedh Slaine*. Retrieved from http://www.maryjones.us/ctexts/aedhslaine.html

Keating, G., (1854) *The History of Ireland*

Keating, G., (1857) *Foras Feasa ar Éirinn*

Kinsella, T., (1969) *The Tain*

Leabhar na h-Uidre (nd). Retrieved from http://www.maryj ones.us/ctexts/flidais.html

Leahy, A., (1906) *Heroic Romances of Ireland*

Macalister, R., (1941) *Lebor Gabala Erenn*, volume 4

Macalister, R., (1956) *Lebor Gabala Erenn*, volume 5

MacKillop, J., (1998) *A Dictionary of Celtic Mythology*

MacNeill, M., (1962) *Festival of Lughnasa*

MacQuarrie, C., (1997) *The Waves of Manannan: A Study of the Literary Representations of Manannan Mac Lir From 'Immram Brian' (c. 700) to 'Finnegan's Wake' (1939)*

Meyer, K., (1906) *The Triads of Ireland*

Monaghan, P., (2004) *Encyclopedia of Celtic Mythology and Folklore*

Murphy, G., (1956) *Early Irish Lyrics: Eighth to Twelfth Centuries*

Nodens (2012) Websters Online Dictionary. http://www.websters-online-dictionary.org/definitions/Nodens

O Donaill (1977) *Focloir Gaeilge-Bearla*

O Grady, H,. (1892) *Silva Gadelica*

O hOgain (2006) *The Lore of Ireland*

Sanas Cormaic., (n.d.) *Three Irish Glossaries*

Shaw, F., (1934) *The Dream of Oengus; Aislinge Oenguso*

Sjoestedt, M. (2000) *Celtic Gods and Heroes*

Smyth, D., (1988) *A Guide to Irish Mythology*

Stokes, W., (1895) *Rennes Dindshenchas*

Stokes, W., (1901) *Thesaurus Palaeohibernicus: A Collection of Old-*

Irish Glosses, Scolia, Prose, and Verse
Stokes, W., (1926) *The Second Battle of Moytura*
Theirling, I., (2001) *More Than Winter's Crone*
Wilde (1991) *Irish Cures, Mystic Charms & Superstitions*
Windisch, E., (1905) *Tain Bo Cuiligne*

Moon Books

PAGANISM & SHAMANISM

What is Paganism? A religion, a spirituality, an alternative
belief system, nature worship? You can find support for all
these definitions (and many more) in dictionaries,
encyclopaedias, and text books of religion, but subscribe to
any one and the truth will evade you. Above all Paganism is a
creative pursuit, an encounter with reality, an exploration of
meaning and an expression of the soul. Druids, Heathens,
Wiccans and others, all contribute their insights and literary
riches to the Pagan tradition. Moon Books invites you to begin
or to deepen your own encounter, right here, right now.
If you have enjoyed this book, why not tell other readers by
posting a review on your preferred book site. Recent
bestsellers from Moon Books are:

Journey to the Dark Goddess
How to Return to Your Soul
Jane Meredith
Discover the powerful secrets of the Dark Goddess and
transform your depression, grief and pain into healing
and integration.
Paperback: 978-1-84694-677-6 ebook: 978-1-78099-223-5

Shamanic Reiki
Expanded Ways of Working with Universal Life Force Energy
Llyn Roberts, Robert Levy
Shamanism and Reiki are each powerful ways of healing;
together, their power multiplies. *Shamanic Reiki* introduces
techniques to help healers and Reiki practitioners tap ancient
healing wisdom.
Paperback: 978-1-84694-037-8 ebook: 978-1-84694-650-9

Pagan Portals - The Awen Alone
Walking the Path of the Solitary Druid
Joanna van der Hoeven
An introductory guide for the solitary Druid, The Awen Alone
will accompany you as you explore, and seek out your own
place within the natural world.
Paperback: 978-1-78279-547-6 ebook: 978-1-78279-546-9

A Kitchen Witch's World of Magical Herbs & Plants
Rachel Patterson
A journey into the magical world of herbs and plants, filled with
magical uses, folklore, history and practical magic. By popular
writer, blogger and kitchen witch, Tansy Firedragon.
Paperback: 978-1-78279-621-3 ebook: 978-1-78279-620-6

Medicine for the Soul
The Complete Book of Shamanic Healing
Ross Heaven
All you will ever need to know about shamanic healing and
how to become your own shaman...
Paperback: 978-1-78099-419-2 ebook: 978-1-78099-420-8

Shaman Pathways - The Druid Shaman
Exploring the Celtic Otherworld
Danu Forest
A practical guide to Celtic shamanism with exercises and
techniques as well as traditional lore for exploring the Celtic
Otherworld.
Paperback: 978-1-78099-615-8 ebook: 978-1-78099-616-5

Traditional Witchcraft for the Woods and Forests
A Witch's Guide to the Woodland with Guided Meditations and
Pathworking
Melusine Draco
A Witch's guide to walking alone in the woods, with guided
meditations and pathworking.
Paperback: 978-1-84694-803-9 ebook: 978-1-84694-804-6

Wild Earth, Wild Soul
A Manual for an Ecstatic Culture
Bill Pfeiffer
Imagine a nature-based culture so alive and so connected,
spreading like wildfire. This book is the first flame...
Paperback: 978-1-78099-187-0 ebook: 978-1-78099-188-7

Naming the Goddess
Trevor Greenfield
Naming the Goddess is written by over eighty adherents and
scholars of Goddess and Goddess Spirituality.
Paperback: 978-1-78279-476-9 ebook: 978-1-78279-475-2

Shapeshifting into Higher Consciousness
Heal and Transform Yourself and Our World with Ancient
Shamanic and Modern Methods
Llyn Roberts
Ancient and modern methods that you can use every day
to transform yourself and make a positive difference in the
world.
Paperback: 978-1-84694-843-5 ebook: 978-1-84694-844-2

Readers of ebooks can buy or view any of these bestsellers by clicking on the live link in the title. Most titles are published in paperback and as an ebook. Paperbacks are available in traditional bookshops. Both print and ebook formats are available online.

Find more titles and sign up to our readers' newsletter at http://www.johnhuntpublishing.com/paganism. Follow us on Facebook at https://www.facebook.com/MoonBooks and Twitter at https://twitter.com/MoonBooksJHP